Collaborative Leadership in Action

A Field Guide for Creating Meetings that Make a Difference

Patrick Sanaghan, Ed.D.
Paulette A. Gabriel, Ed.D.

HRD Press, Inc. • Amherst • Massachusetts

Published by: HRD Press, Inc.
                22 Amherst Road
                Amherst, MA 01002
                413-253-3488
                800-822-2801 (U.S. and Canada)
                413-253-3490 (fax)
                www.hrdpress.com

ISBN 978-1-59996-252-8

Editorial services by Sally M. Farnham
Production services by Jean S. Miller
Cover design by Eileen Klockars

— Contents —

Collaborative Leadership in Action:
A Field Guide for Creating Meetings that Make a Difference

Design Index

Design Name	Page	Level of Difficulty			Time Required			
		Easy	Moderate	Challenging	30–60 Min.	1–2 Hrs.	2–3 Hrs.	> 3 Hrs.
Affinity Diagram	97	✓			✓			
Carousel Design	25	✓			✓			
Cascading Agreement	31	✓			✓			
Collaborative Teaching Design	103		✓			✓		
Creating Group Connections	165		✓	✓		✓		
Customer/Stakeholder Feedback	51			✓		✓		
Interview Design	39			✓		✓		
Engaged Problem Solving	69		✓			✓		
Metaphorical Problem Solving	89			✓	✓			
New Leader Assimilation	173		✓			✓		
Open Space	115			✓				✓
Panel Discussion	125		✓			✓	✓	✓
Solutions Matrix	83		✓			✓		
Systems Perspective	133		✓	✓		✓		
Team Effectiveness Check-In	179	✓				✓		
Team Operating Ground Rules	153	✓				✓		
Team "Talent Audit"	147	✓			✓			
Team Transition Design	157		✓			✓		
The Future Timeline	109		✓			✓		
The Pre-Mortem	75			✓		✓		
Trauma Clinic	61			✓			✓	

— Acknowledgments —

Patrick Sanaghan would like to acknowledge the contribution of Dr. Nancy Aronson, a colleague and friend, in the original conceptualization of this Systems Perspective design. She has taught us more about collaborative work than any other colleague.

He would also like to acknowledge Dr. Rod Napier, the originator of the Interview Design and a former mentor.

Patrick Sanaghan and Paulette Gabriel want to thank Diane Gardner for her exceptional support with this project. She helped to make it happen and we are in her debt.

— Introduction —

Collaborative Leadership

In a complex world—where most problems can't be solved without collaboration, where most outcomes are shared, and where decision paths are dense and dispersed—being able to deliver key outcomes across organizational boundaries makes the difference between success and failure. Leaders who understand how to generate passion, participation, and results are few and far between. Working from previous paradigms, most leaders don't really know that "Collaboration needs a different kind of leadership; it needs leaders who can safeguard the process, facilitate interaction and patiently deal with high levels of frustration" (Chrislip, 2002).

This book is meant to inform and guide leaders, consultants, human resource professionals, and others in creating meaningful engagement and connection, especially in meetings. The difference between a productive climate and one that is mediocre is vast. How can leaders systematically create a climate that fosters the kind of focus, psychological safety, and inclusion that result in superior performance and satisfaction? We aim to shine a light on ways you can use group settings to focus the work, create interpersonal support and collaboration, and empower employees to take action and make decisions.

When everyone's role is to create the climate for people to do their best work with passion, commitment, and energy, not only does everyone win, the organization wins, the leaders or customers they serve win, and the shareholders win. Our goal is to provide leaders, consultants, trainers, and others with the tools and approaches that escalate the power and importance of meetings so that instead of being a time and energy drain, meetings form the fundamental architecture for intentional engagement, purposeful learning, and action-oriented connection.

The Five Fundamentals

The framework for the designs, tools, and approaches we are sharing with you are founded in key principles that really matter when it comes to building a community, a team, or an organization of empowered people. The five fundamentals are

1. **Being intentional.** Being effective, engaging, and collaborative does not happen simply by chance. You can't put a group of smart people in a room and hope something wonderful happens. When leaders, consultants, trainers, and others take on the challenge of intentional engagement, the action step is to adopt a design mentality as a crucial element in creating processes and approaches that focus the effort toward the right goals.

2. **Building trust.** Without trust, there is little chance of engagement. One of the key mistakes people make is to assume that trust is a given. Part of being intentional is building a reputation and climate for honest and transparent communication, fulfilling promises and agreements, and providing a venue for addressing issues that are sticky, difficult, and hidden. Constructing ways to address trust that results in a culture and climate that enable higher levels of participation, performance, and capability is at the heart of good design and good meetings. Effective meeting designs can build trust throughout an organization. This book will show you how to do this.

3. **Being inclusive.** When people feel like an outsider, they will not be engaged. When they don't feel heard, they will not be connected. Good meetings connect with diverse learning styles, focus on engaging every mind, and give people a sense of belonging. These collaborative meeting designs ensure that all voices will be heard in an organization without becoming overwhelmed with complexity or information overload.

4. **Creating alignment.** People are more engaged when their sense of alignment with their organization's vision and values are apparent and explicit. The connection between what they do and the bigger picture is the glue of high performance. Gaining a group or team commitment to being aligned is a never-ending responsibility and does not occur through osmosis or a one-shot deal. Holding frequent and intentional meetings creates the ongoing focus that gets the job done quicker and with more effectiveness and commitment.

5. **Developing the team.** Effective leaders, consultants, and trainers understand the potential for significant increases in performance through high-performing teams. They make sure that all team members understand the strengths they and other team members bring to the team and work at developing a process that capitalizes on all of these strengths. Many of the designs in this book will show you how to build and maintain a stellar organizational team.

The Concept of Design

The term *design* refers to the "creative process of planning and facilitating a set of activities that move a group successfully and transparently toward conscious goals" (Sanaghan, 2009). The concept crops up repeatedly in our daily lives. If you wanted to give a birthday party for a close friend, you might invite specific guests who are close to the birthday boy or girl, arrange for upbeat music, plan some fun activities, decorate your home with balloons and other festive items, and order a birthday cake. You'd carefully and intentionally plan all of the details to achieve your desired outcome of celebrating your friend's birthday.

Now imagine that you had the unfortunate task of planning a memorial service for the same friend. Although many of the same elements from the birthday party might be present, you would organize, or design, them very differently. The same people might attend, but their dress would be somber, not festive. The music would be subdued rather than upbeat. You might serve food, but rather than being a centerpiece for the gathering, it would be for sustenance only. The decorations would be conservative and respectful, the colors muted rather than bright.

Same friend, same people attending—but because of the circumstances, the two events would be designed and organized very differently. Similarly, every opportunity to collaborate has myriad details to think through and organize based on the desired outcome.

The Four Elements of Collaborative Design

Four key elements come into play when you want to create interactive and collaborative meetings. They are

1. **Purpose.** What do you want to accomplish? Clarifying the purpose is the most important thing you can do because it drives everything else that you do to organize a collaborative outcome-based meeting.

   To zero in on your purpose, it may help to answer these questions:

   - Am I deciding something or seeking input from participants?
   - Am I trying to prioritize a set of planning recommendations?
   - Do I want to share information with people and then solicit feedback?
   - Do I want to openly discuss a sensitive topic or gather data about it?
   - Do I have a problem I need help in solving, or do I want to provide a solution and test its soundness with others?
   - Do I want participants to tap their creative potential? Provide ideas? Perspective?
   - Do I want participants to share their accomplishments or their concerns?

   The answer to each question would point to different purposes. For instance, deciding something is different than discussing. Prioritizing is different than discussing a sensitive topic. Each of these different purposes would call for a different set of activities or designs that would move you toward your articulated goals.

   As you think about outcomes you want to achieve, also think of the process goals you want to authentically accomplish. How do you want people to feel about the experience? You might, for instance, want to make sure people authentically feel as if their contributions were valued, that they had a chance to truly participate and influence the ideas of others, and that the meeting created a sense of community. It's not necessary to communicate the process goals to attendees, but you should think them through carefully.

   Once you have determined the meeting's purpose, you can begin thinking about the other three key elements to creating collaboration. Without a clearly understood and articulated purpose, everything else will suffer.

2. **Stakeholders.** After defining the purpose(s), ask "Who will advance your purpose?" "Who has a stake in the meeting?" and "Whose participation is essential?" Think about those individuals or groups who could either help you with their participation or hurt you if they aren't a part of things.

   If you want to solve a complex problem, for instance, you may want participants who have some experience with the problem, who could be affected by the problem, or who can provide creative ideas and approaches to the problem. These may be three distinct stakeholder groups. To have a full conversation about organizational communication, you need to identify representatives from a variety of stakeholder groups, such as administrative professionals, field salespeople, operations employees, and communication experts.

   Every company has scores of potential stakeholders. The challenge is to determine what stakeholders must be involved in a particular meeting. Many organizations fall into the trap of inviting everyone to everything rather than being conscious and intentional about the attendee list. But if the same set of players always gets together to solve organizational problems, their view will be narrow and unchanging.

3. **Design.** As noted above, focus on organizing the meeting so that it realizes your intended outcomes. Think through the set of questions related to determining purpose and figure out the kinds of activities that will help engage participants and get the job done.

   For a reality check, bounce your ideas off several colleagues. Explain what you want to accomplish, who will attend, and how you intend to achieve the intended results. Your colleagues will help you identify the strengths and weaknesses of your design so that you can better prepare for the meeting. Inform the leader of what design or set of designs you'll use so that there won't be any surprises.

4. **Logistics.** Logistics refers to all the physical things that help support the discussions, dialogues, and learning experiences that the meeting is designed to produce. These range from the space and set-up of the meeting room to which items participants may need to complete their work.

Before the meeting occurs, visit the room you will be using to get a feel for its strengths and weaknesses. A diagram is rarely helpful. Because many collaborative activities use flip chart paper, look for adequate wall space on which to post the paper. Many meeting rooms in offices have beautiful pictures, sconces, and curtains on the walls; hanging paper in such a room is difficult.

Ensure that you have enough space for people to feel comfortable moving around. Collaborative activities, which are designed for maximum interaction and participation, encourage a lot of movement. You can always make a large room smaller by rearranging flip charts and chairs, but a small, cramped room cannot be enlarged. Bigger is almost always better.

On the day of the meeting, show up early so that you will have time to fix anything that may seem wrong with the physical arrangement and other details. Here's why: We once had a meeting schedule for more than 100 participants. When we asked to look over the room beforehand, the leader replied, "You will love the room. It's large and can hold almost 200 people. There's not enough time to see it because we have a lot to do today."

We never saw the room, much to our chagrin. When we showed up the next day to facilitate the meeting, we entered a large ballroom with six beautiful but large pillars that blocked everyone's view. The room was a great place to eat—but not to meet.

The Rule of Four

This rule is one of the most powerful ideas in group and organizational development. This concept creates the context for utilizing small groups, designing for participation and engagement, and raising our awareness about the impact of a small group of individuals in a meeting. **Never forget this rule.**

The Rule of Four tells us that in a group of 10 to 40+ people, four to five individuals will do 80 percent of the talking! Just think about that for a minute: we didn't say the smartest people would dominate a meeting, it would be the overly verbal ones who will!

This is one of the important reasons we have to organize or "design" a meeting so that we hear from everyone, not just the four who tend to take over.

In many meetings, there are different levels of power in the room (e.g., staff, senior vice presidents, directors) **or** a few "experts" who overly share their expertise **or** older participants who tend to dominate younger people. Unless you carefully think through how to meaningfully engage everyone in the room, the dominant people will run the meeting.

We don't want to shut down the four or five dominate personalities, but we do want to neutralize their impact. All the meeting designs in this book take the Rule of Four into deep consideration. They will allow **all** the participants in a meeting to share their ideas and passions.

By the way, the people who tend to dominate a meeting or group do not like the Rule of Four. They realize that if we utilize small groups, they will not be able to control things, hold the stage, or bully participants into agreement.

Guiding Principles

What makes these collaborative meeting designs so effective is that they maintain the following principles:

1. **They are all battled tested.** We have used these in the corporate sector, in the nonprofit arena, and in higher education. Our clients have included Cornell University, Independence Blue Cross Insurance, The Pennsylvania Horticultural Society, Shell Oil, Barclay Capital, Saudi Aramco, Saint Joseph's University, FMC, and Central Community College.

   We have worked in hundreds of organizations over the past 25 years, utilizing these designs to solve tough problems, build community and ownership, help create strategy, and most importantly, tap the creative resources of organizations and get things done. They work.

2. **They are user friendly.** Most of the meeting designs presented in this book are easy to implement and execute. There are a few that are challenging, but with careful planning and a little support, most people can do them.

   In many ways, this is like a good cookbook. If you follow the directions carefully, identify the purposes and goals of a particular meeting, and apply the right meeting design, you will be successful.

3. **They are transparent.** Meeting participants can clearly see and understand what is taking place in the meeting. There are no hidden agendas or manipulation. The meeting designs support the agreed-upon outcome (e.g., make a decision, diagnose a problem, brainstorm a solution). The design does not drive people toward a specific solution or decision that has already been made. Let's repeat that: *You cannot use these designs to make people "feel involved."* Meaningful participation of meeting participants is what matters. Their participation is only successful if they can influence the final outcome.

   For leaders, this is especially important to remember. More than a few times we have been asked by senior leaders to "do something that makes people feel like the already agreed-upon solution was theirs." Obviously, we turned down the opportunity, but it is not as rare as you might think.

   Transparency is a double-edged sword. When you meaningfully engage people and when there is no hidden agenda, you cannot predict the outcome. You have to trust that the meeting participants have the knowledge, expertise, and aspiration to produce the appropriate outcome. You cannot suddenly change course during the meeting if it isn't going your way.

4. **They take into account and utilize different learning styles.** We will talk a lot about learning styles later in the book, but it is important to note that in any meeting, there are diverse learning styles present. Some participants seek a lot of interaction with others, some want to use their imagination and creativity, and others want facts, details, and structure. No one style is better than another, but they are all present—*in every meeting.*

   These designs take the different learning styles into consideration in conscious ways, which enables everyone to contribute meaningfully to the meeting's goals and purposes.

5. **They promote and support participation and interaction.** The challenge for any facilitator or leader of a meeting is to ensure that all the voices are heard, not just the dominant ones. Shy and quiet people will rarely speak in a group of 30 or 40 people. These designs utilize small groups that promote participant interaction and contribution.

We realize that some people don't like small groups because they feel "touchy feely." None of these meeting designs are touchy feely. They all produce clear outcomes and have definitive and appropriate structure.

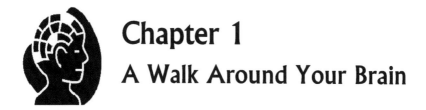

Chapter 1
A Walk Around Your Brain

People view the world from drastically different perspectives. It is a fascinating concept and one we examine in-depth by first presenting the following different constructs about thinking styles, then through our "commonsensical" model. Connecting to those diverse styles in a meeting environment allows the meeting to produce important and relevant outcomes for all involved.

The Benziger Thinking Style Assessment (BTSA)

This assessment identifies four very different modes of thinking that will help determine how and why people see the world differently:

- Frontal Left—logical thinkers
- Frontal Right—powerful visual thinkers
- Basal Left—prefers logical order
- Basal Right—feelings-based

Herrmann Brain Dominance Instrument (HBDI)

This is a model that displays four different "thinking styles" that help us perceive how different types of thinkers view the world.

- A Quadrant—rational
- B Quadrant—self-keeping
- C Quadrant—feeling
- D Quadrant—experimental

Anthony Gregorc Thinking Styles

In this model, individuals explore their different ways of thinking, learning, and behaving.

- Concrete Sequential
- Concrete Random
- Abstract Sequential
- Abstract Random

David Kolb's Learning Styles Model

The connection between how we think and how we learn is stronger than many know. This model suggests that four distinct learning styles, based on a four-stage cycle, create the framework for learning situations that can touch everyone and satisfy diverse group expectations.

Commonsensical Thinking Style Model (CTSM)

We use our **CTSM** model to create, craft, plan, and design the meetings we facilitate for maximum effectiveness and what considerations that need to take into account when developing the meeting agenda and plan. The main principle is the more learning styles utilized in meeting designs, the more holistic *and* effective the meetings become.

The Evolution of a "Commonsensical" Model

In this chapter, we'll outline what has helped to shape the "commonsensical" model that informs our thinking when we go to organize or "design" a meeting. It's important to realize that in a meeting of 10, 50, or even 100 people, there will be a rich diversity of thinking styles and needs. In crafting the meeting, attention to different styles taps the talent and gifts of participants. Each style brings and produces meaningful outcomes that all participants can appreciate.

The following different constructs about thinking systems have helped inform and influence our thinking about how people see and experience the world. These styles represent sometimes dramatically different perspectives.

The Benziger Thinking Style Assessment (BTSA)

The Benziger Thinking Style Assessment (BTSA) identifies four modes of thinking:

Frontal Left

- Logical thinkers
- Very good at math
- Have a diagnostic mentality
- Like structured analysis
- Can generate efficient solutions
- Like well-defined goals

Frontal Right

- Powerful visual thinkers
- Think metaphorically
- Conceptual thinkers
- Imaginative
- Integrate concepts easily
- Spatial thinkers

Basal Left

- Prefer procedures
- Orderly approach to things
- Like established procedures and routines
- Enjoy details
- Thorough
- Like step-by-step problem solving
- Like completing tasks

Basal Right

- Spiritual, symbolic, feeling-based
- Highly expressive
- Like to connect with others
- Feelings are important
- Supportive of others
- Relationships are very important to them

As you can see, the four modes of thinking are very different! Imagine for a minute that you have a group that is half frontal left and half basal right. They will want very different things from the meeting. The challenge is how do you create or "design" a meeting to meet their unique expectations, needs, and styles?

Anthony Gregorc

Another helpful framework is Professor Anthony Gregorc's work that identifies four different types of thinking styles:

1. **Concrete sequential.** These individuals process information in an orderly, sequential, and linear fashion. They like to break tasks into specific steps. They notice details, appreciate specific information, and tend to be reality based.

13

2. **Concrete random.** These individuals are experimenters and like to find alternative ways of doing things and solving problems. A trial-and-error approach is fine with them, and they appreciate multiple perspectives and viewpoints. They also like to do things their way.

3. **Abstract sequential.** These individuals love the world of ideas and abstract thought. They love to read and are thorough researchers. They often like to work alone and appreciate structure in work situations. They are intellectual, rational, and logical in their thinking.

4. **Abstract random.** These individuals organize information through reflection. They thrive in unstructured, people-orientated environments. They remember personalized information and are comfortable with their own and other's feelings and emotions. They are not fond of structure and are visual learners. They love colors.

With Gregorc's model, you can see that individuals have very different ways of thinking, learning, and behaving. Some people are quite linear in their thinking, others need time to reflect, and still others like to experiment with ideas. All these different ways of being are in your meeting! The challenge, then, is how do you utilize the great gifts these individuals bring to the table, engage them meaningfully, and actually accomplish something everyone buys into?

Herrmann Brain Dominance Instrument (HBDI)

The Herrmann Brain Dominance Instrument (HBDI) is a validated instrument and one of our favorite models for showing the dramatic differences of how people perceive the world and how they think.

The HBDI's four thinking styles are:

A Quadrant (Rational Self)

- Critical
- Logical
- Quantify
- Analyzes
- Know how things work
- Realistic
- Like numbers/money/data
- Measure carefully
- Precise

D Quadrant (Experimental Self)

- Take risks
- Imagine
- Like surprises
- Curious
- Make connections
- Break rules
- Integrate ideas
- See big picture
- Synthesize

B Quadrant (Self-Keeping Self)

- Plan well
- On time
- Get things done
- Reliable
- Organized/orderly
- Neat
- Stable
- Establish order and structure
- Practical problem solver

C Quadrant (Feeling Self)

- Talk a lot
- Express feelings
- Emotional
- Expressive
- Like to teach
- Sensitive to others
- Supportive
- Share with others
- Relationship focused

David Kolb's Learning Styles Model

The connection between how we think and how we learn is strong. Since meetings are grounded in learning and developing, David Kolb's learning styles model can be instrumental in targeting learning situations that work for everyone. Kolb's learning styles model suggests that four distinct learning styles based on a four-stage learning cycle frame the way in which we can create learning situations that touch all four preferences or styles.

Experiencing, reflecting, thinking, and acting are the four preferences that form a four-stage cycle:

1. Concrete Experience (CE) Feeling
2. Reflective Observation (RO) Watching
3. Abstract Conceptualization (AC) Thinking
4. Active Experimentation (AE) Doing

The four-type definition of learning styles is each a combination of two preferred styles. They are:

1. Diverging (CE/RO)
2. Assimilating (AC/RO)
3. Converging (AC/AE)
4. Accommodating (CE/AE)

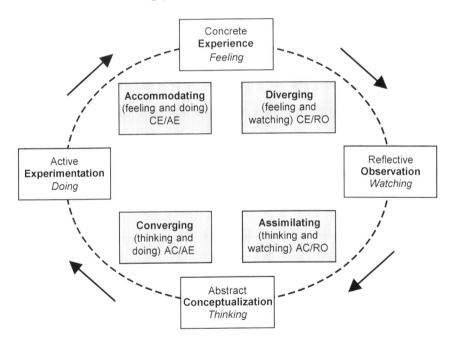

Although different people naturally prefer a learning style, the ability to integrate all four different learning styles improves as we mature through development stages.

Here are brief descriptions of the four Kolb learning styles:

Diverging (feeling and watching—CE/RO)

- Able to look at things from different perspectives
- Are sensitive
- Prefer to watch rather than do
- Tend to gather information and use imagination to solve problems
- Are best at viewing concrete situations from several different viewpoints
- Have broad cultural interests
- Like to gather information
- Are interested in people
- Are imaginative and emotional
- Are strong in the arts
- Prefers to work in groups
- Listen with an open mind
- Receive personal feedback

Assimilating (thinking and watching—AC/RO)

- Use concise, logical approach
- Think ideas and concepts are more important than people
- Require a good, clear explanation rather than practical opportunity
- Excel at understanding wide-ranging information and organize it in a clear, logical format
- Are less focused on people and more interested in abstract concepts and ideas
- Are more attracted to logically sound theories than practical value-based approaches
- Prefer reading, listening to lectures, exploring analytical models, and having time to think things through

Converging (thinking and doing—AC/AE)

- Can solve problems using their learning to find solutions to practical issues
- Prefer technical tasks
- Are less concerned with people and interpersonal aspects

- Are best at finding practical uses for ideas and theories
- Make decisions by finding solutions to questions and problems
- Are more attracted to technical tasks and problems than social or interpersonal issues
- Enable specialist and technology abilities
- Like to experiment with new ideas and to simulate and work with practical applications

Accommodating (doing and feeling—AE/CE)

- Are "hands-on," relying on intuition rather than logic
- Use other people's analysis and prefer to take a practical, experiential approach
- Are attracted to new challenges and experiences and to carrying out plans
- Commonly act on "gut" instinct rather than logical analysis
- Tend to rely on others for information rather than carry out their own analysis
- Are prevalent and useful in roles requiring action and initiative
- Prefer to work in teams to complete tasks
- Set targets and actively work in the field, trying different ways to achieve an objective

Again, a good meeting design for diverse thinking types would have experiential, reflective, conceptual, and action-oriented segments. One strength in creating this kind of meeting enables maturations through the learning cycle.

A Commonsensical Thinking Style Model (CTSM)
(Sanaghan, 2011)

The following *informal* model is based on common sense and is one way to look at people's different thinking styles and, more importantly, help describe what people want a meeting to look like. It is critical that leaders and facilitators deeply understand the very different expectations participants will have at meetings they are trying to facilitate. Here, we have integrated the best of the thinking style constructs to frame what you need to consider in terms of thinking and learning styles. We have narrowed it down to four basic types:

Analytics

- Very conscious of time
- Like information, data facts
- Logical
- Rational
- Like order and predictability
- Details matter!
- Good with math
- They ask: *What are the facts and are they accurate?*

Possibilities

- See connections
- Tolerate ambiguity well
- Visionary
- Love ideas/theories
- Possibility thinkers
- Creativity is prized
- Tend to be optimistic
- They ask: *What are the possibilities?*

Practicals

- Task oriented
- Conscious of time
- Prize structure/format
- Like agendas
- Complete tasks/achievers
- Concrete thinkers
- Like control
- No interruptions, are respectful
- Direct/frank/forceful
- Results oriented
- Practical
- They ask: ***How*** *will we do this and* ***who*** *will do it?*

Relators

- Relating and connecting to others is key
- Process is important
- Listening conveys respect—feeling heard is a priority
- Emotions are respected and expected
- Stories are great
- Getting everyone on same page is important
- They ask: *Is the process fair? Do people feel included?*

What the Different Thinkers Want in a Meeting

Analytics

- A clear, short, and *prioritized* agenda distributed *before* the meeting is essential—no agenda = no meeting.
- One hour maximum is needed for a meeting; 30 minutes is usually plenty of time.
- Any pre-work (e.g., research, reports, information) needs to be distributed *before* the meeting and read by everyone who is attending—always come prepared.
- Be on time; lateness is disrespectful.
- Tangents are not needed—they waste time.
- Get to the point—speeches are not needed or wanted.
- Use facts and logic to support your arguments—emotions and "feelings" don't matter.
- Brainstorming is not welcome.
- The facilitator's job is to make sure participants adhere to the agenda and especially the timeframes allotted for each agenda item.
- Minutes should be brief and turned around quickly—any assignments need to be identified.

Practicals

- An agenda is essential—please follow the sequence (tangents are not appreciated).
- The facilitator's role is to keep things on track.
- An hour is plenty of time for a meeting—more is wasteful.
- Focus on results, results, results.
- Speak to the agenda—minimal brainstorming is allowed.
- Get to the point—don't waste people's time.
- Always keep in mind that the nuts and bolts really matter.
- Be on time, end on time; anything less is failure.
- Identify who does what and when before participants leave the meeting—leave no loose ends.

Relators

- They love personal interaction, conversation, and sharing with others.
- It is important that participants "feel" heard.
- Use stories and/or metaphors to communicate your ideas.
- Take your time to express yourself.
- Listening to others is very important.
- Likes energizers and ice breakers that enable you to get to know others.
- Don't start until everyone is present.
- Agendas are okay, but not essential.
- The facilitator's job is to make sure everyone is involved in the discussion and that people are listened to.
- It is helpful to go around and hear from everyone about what they like or appreciated about the meeting.
- Round tables are preferred so that participants can see everyone— comfortable chairs are essential.
- A minimum of an hour for a meeting—two hours is best.
- First half of the meeting is to get to know each other and connect, the second half is to share ideas.

Possibilities

- Ideas are the currency of a possibilities meeting—the more the better. Tangents and brainstorming are welcomed.
- Criticism is not needed—generativity is sought after.
- It could take an hour just to get warmed up! Time does not drive a meeting—it can constrain it.
- Imagination and creativity are encouraged—there are no "bad" ideas.
- As long as participants know the purpose of the meeting, agendas only get in the way.
- Build on each other's ideas.
- A facilitator is not needed; participants can self-facilitate.
- The physical space needs to support interaction—lots of whiteboards, markers, flip charts, windows.

As you can see, participants have very different wants, needs, and expectations about meetings they participate in. All the designs in this book attempt to meaningfully connect with the four distinct thinking styles. You will find creative ways of engaging people *(Possibilities and Relators)*, produce quality information *(Analytics)* and create credible, specific outcomes *(Practicals)*.

We use our CTSM to create, craft, plan, and design the meetings we facilitate. As you read the different designs, consciously focus on this. The more learning styles you utilize in the meeting designs, the more holistic *and* effective they are.

We will identify these connections from time to time so that you can see how our CTSM influences each design.

Thinking Styles Scorecard

A collaborative meeting needs to meaningfully involve as many different thinking styles as possible. The very best "designs" in this book meaningfully touch all four styles. Not every meeting needs to touch every style. For example, if you are beginning a brainstorming session about solving a problem, this will play to the Analytics because they can generate lots of information and the Possibilities because they can offer creative ideas. It probably won't engage the Relators as much as the other two, and the Practicals can get overwhelmed with too much data.

To somewhat connect with the Practicals, use a multivoting technique like the Las Vegas Voting (refer to the Toolbox section) to *prioritize* the ideas from the brainstorming list.

To connect a little with the Relators, you could have participants do a "pair and share" before they call out their ideas. A pair and share involves two people talking with each other for one to two minutes to stimulate thinking *before* they participate in the group discussion.

At some level, each design we have in the book takes all four styles into consideration; however, specific designs really connect to specific thinking styles. We will indicate the primary styles each design addresses at the very beginning of each description of the design.

Chapter 2
Data Gathering

Meetings can only be effective if they engage participants in an inclusive way. Gathering data and feedback not only helps achieve goals and encourage progress, it creates a diagnostic climate that encourages critical thinking, effective problem solving, and healthy debate. These various designs help meeting leaders collect information and assess it in an organized, effective way that leads to better overall communication, connection, and collaboration.

Carousel Design

This design encourages group interaction as participants go through a process designed to gather information about a variety of key topics. The process draws out points of view, supports equal and inclusive participation, and underscores the importance of considering multiple perspectives when looking at a problem, an issue, or an opportunity. The resulting ideas are shared openly to help bring about positive change, with a unique outcome every time.

Cascading Agreement

This activity is intended to increase collaboration and commitment among employees. Small groups are formed to facilitate discussion and allow all voices to be heard. The objectives are prioritize key issues, enable open exchange, facilitate large groups' communication, and eventually agree on ways to address what has been developed.

Interview Design

This is one of the most powerful and engaging meeting designs available and can create a stakeholder database that has been sourced from a wide variety of people. Large groups with as many as 100 people will work together, openly sharing ideas and information and coming up with strategies to solve various problems. With a focus on themes, groups can see how their generative work evolves right then and there—that is the power of this design.

Customer/Stakeholder Feedback

This exercise is an adaptation of the "Fishbowl" exercise and requires the talents of a good group facilitator. The discussion revolves around how to respond effectively to customers, but is flexible enough to use among a variety of different groups. Through a series of interactions where the responses are explored in the moment by the participants, this approach results in clear and shared commitments and a sense of collective and transparent participation.

 # Carousel Design

Level of Difficulty: Easy

Estimated Time: 45–50 minutes

Thinking Styles Utilized: Analytics, Practicals, Relators, Possibilities

Synopsis:

This highly interactive collaborative meeting design can be used effectively to gather information about significant topics (such as organizational climate, ways to enhance communication, and how to generate ideas for improvement). Its greatest value is its transparency: ideas are shared openly, and no one can control the outcome.

We will use the Carousel as a vehicle to conduct a SWOT (Strengths, Weaknesses, Opportunities, Threats) analysis.

Goals:

1. To fully involve all meeting participants
2. To create a prioritized database in a short period of time

Logistics:

Materials: Flip chart paper, easels, a magic marker for every participant, masking tape, timer, and chimes (or a bell)

Space Needs: Large, comfortable room where participants can move around easily, plus a lot of usable wall space

Number of Participants: 10 to 40 (Using 40 participants as the example, create four mixed groups of participants by having people count off from one to four. This will produce four groups of 10 people each. Clearly label and number the four focus questions on four different flip charts posted around the room.)

Your room should look like this:

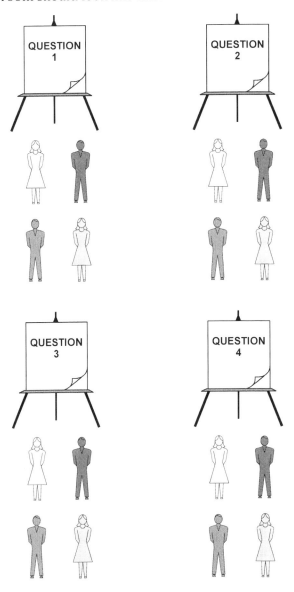

For large groups of 40, have several flip charts at each station so that people do not have to wait for others to finish writing their ideas. You can also tape extra flip chart paper on the walls near each station to enable several people to write simultaneously.

The Activity:

1. Ask participants to go to the station that represents the number they were assigned (e.g., 1, 2, 3, 4).

2. Instruct each group to read the focus question at their assigned station and individually record their responses directly on the flip chart. Make sure every participant has a magic marker. Say:

    > "This is not about group agreement. We want individual responses. If you agree with another person's ideas, indicate your agreement by checking (✓) the idea."

3. Give each group about five minutes to read the focus question and individually record responses. Discourage people from talking or debating an idea on the flip chart. Encourage individual responses.

4. At the end of the allotted time, use a bell or chimes to signal that it's time for each group to move clockwise to the next station. Make sure everyone stays with their group while the rotation occurs.

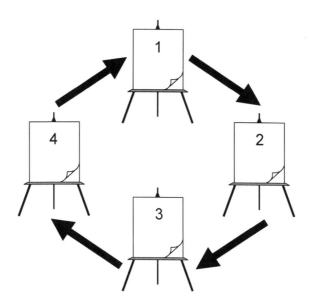

5. Ask participants to read the previous group's input, individually check off the ideas with which they agree, and *add their own ideas* to the list.

6. Continue the rotation until all four groups have visited all four stations and individually recorded their responses.

7. Have each group return to its original question. A lot of new information will have been added to their original responses. Give them several minutes to read the new information and check off the answers with which they agree.

Facilitator Tip:

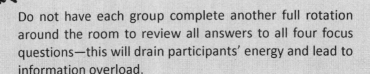

Do not have each group complete another full rotation around the room to review all answers to all four focus questions—this will drain participants' energy and lead to information overload.

8. Ask each original group to report the top four or five answers to their focus questions. These will be easily recognized by the check marks. Limit the reports to one or two minutes.

9. Tell participants that all the information created will be captured in electronic form and sent to them.

The SWOT Analysis for ABC Corporation might look like this:

STRENGTHS
Great leadership ✓✓✓✓✓✓✓
Strong regional reputation ✓✓✓✓✓✓✓✓✓✓✓✓
High-functioning board ✓✓✓
We value our customers and clients ✓✓✓✓✓✓✓✓✓✓✓
Quality of our products ✓✓✓✓✓✓✓✓✓

WEAKNESSES
Location is too remote ✓✓✓✓✓✓✓✓✓✓✓
Technology is becoming outdated ✓✓✓✓✓✓
Our reputation is mainly regional ✓✓

OPPORTUNITIES
Population with investment dollars increasing
dramatically ✓✓✓✓✓✓
Interest in personal/expert service is growing ✓✓
Increased use of more stable financial vehicles ✓✓✓✓

THREATS
Other companies have leading edge technology ✓✓✓✓✓✓
Strong competition—larger firms ✓✓✓✓✓
Volatile financial markets ✓✓✓

SCHEDULE	
Facilitator welcomes participants, shares purposes, and gives directions for activity	5 minutes
Facilitator uses a counting-off method to create randomly mixed groups	5 minutes
The four groups answer the focus questions and rotate to all stations	20 minutes
Groups return to their original question, read the information, and check ideas with which they agree	5 minutes
Each group selects the top four or five ideas/answers for their focus question and prepares a brief presentation	5 minutes
Each small group gives a short presentation about its top four or five answers to their question	5 minutes
Facilitator thanks participants and explains how the information will be used	2–3 minutes
Total Time:	**45–50 minutes**

Cascading Agreement

Level of Difficulty: Easy

Estimated Time: 45–60 minutes

Thinking Styles Utilized: Analytics, Practicals, Relators, Possibilities

Synopsis:

There are many situations that require a group of people to discuss real concerns and come to closure with a unified point of view. The Cascading Agreement is especially geared to generate involvement, stimulate vibrant discussion, and create a going forward position. For example, you may have a situation where some stakeholders do not feel valued. As a leader, you want to tackle the issue and gather ideas on how to quickly improve morale. Or perhaps there is an important initiative coming up and you want to prepare your team to address it with a well-thought-out frame of reference and substantive questions. The Cascading Agreement is a perfect design to capture diverse ideas, enable everyone's voice to be heard, create really good generative ideas—all in a short period of time!

Goals:

1. To involve all participants
2. To hear multiple and diverse points of view
3. To increase collaboration and commitment
4. To quickly produce a quality list of ideas

Logistics:

Materials: Flip chart paper, easels, markers

Space Needs: Large, comfortable room with enough space for groups to have discreet conversations

Number of Participants: 10 to 50

The Activity:

In this example, we will use a group of 24 diverse individuals and begin by creating eight groups of three. The use of a small group ensures that all three members will participate. In larger groups of six or eight, one or two people can easily disappear during a discussion dominated by the most verbal participants.

Your room might look like this:

Clarify the purpose of the meeting up front. For example, "We are gathered here today to look at ways we can further improve company morale. We want and need your ideas, and we want to hear from everyone." Explain that the planning design has four specific steps, but don't tell participants more than that. If you walk them through all four steps up front, they will want to get to the end as fast as possible.

Step 1: Create. Ask each group of three to brainstorm eight to ten ways to improve company morale. Emphasize that the quantity of ideas is important, so participants shouldn't be judgmental in this phase of the meeting design.

- Offer some suggestions to give participants an idea of what you are asking (for instance, offer free parking, have lunch with the CEO, and develop employee recognition programs).

- Ask each group to appoint someone to record the ideas, and then give the groups about seven or eight minutes to work.

Step 2: Condense. Ask each group to reduce its list to the top three ideas generated during brainstorming. Explain that this step requires discipline and rigor in deciding what three ideas would best improve company morale. Allocate a couple of minutes for this task. If you give more time, people tend to debate, hold onto their ideas, and talk too much. The tight timeframe gently prods them to produce the best ideas.

- Be on guard for clustering ideas or merging several ideas into one detailed recommendation. For example, the recommendation "We should provide employee-of-the-month awards, along with a monetary reward, and have the CEO present these at an employee lunch" actually contains three ideas.

- Initially, the eight groups will have generated 60 to 70 ways to improve company morale.

- Now, the groups need to agree on the best three to four ideas for their small group. Remember, they will reduce the lists again in the next step.

Step 3: Collaborate. Ask each small group to connect with another small group, creating four groups of six participants. Their task is to share their best ideas with each other and agree on the three very best ideas.

Step 4: Communicate. After each group has agreed on its three best ideas, capture those recommendations on a flip chart in full view of all participants. Take one idea from each group of six, using a round-robin approach. Avoid taking all the ideas from Group 1 and then from Group 2; by the time you get to Group 3, they may feel as if they have nothing new or meaningful to share. Make as many rounds as necessary to record all the ideas on the flip chart.

At this stage, your list might look like the flip chart here:

How to Improve Company Morale

1. Have company-wide picnics/events twice a year
2. Establish an employee recognition program
3. Establish "chat and chews" with the president to discuss issues of importance to employees
4. Have "dress down" Fridays during the summer months
5. Bring in outside experts to teach us how to improve morale
6. Make team building available to everyone
7. Develop a "coaching culture" that rewards innovation

Use a multivoting technique, such as Las Vegas Voting (see page 191) to decide which ideas are the best. This simple prioritization process is completely transparent in its implementation. Give each participant five sticky dots (found at any stationery or office supply store). Explain that these dots represent votes. Participants can place their votes next to the ideas on the master list they believe are best. They can weigh their votes any way they would like. For example, they can place five dots on one idea, put two votes on one idea and three on another, or use one vote for each of five different ideas.

As the participants come up to the flip chart and vote for their favorite ideas, you'll soon see priorities emerging on the list.

Your list might look like this:

How to Improve Company Morale

1. Have company-wide picnics/events twice a year ●●●●●
2. Establish an employee recognition program ●●●●●●●●●●●●●●
3. Establish "chat and chews" with the president to discuss issues of importance to employees ●●●●●●●●●●
4. Have "dress down" Fridays during the summer months ●●
5. Bring in outside experts to teach us how to improve morale ●●
6. Make team building available to everyone ●●●
7. Develop a "coaching culture" that rewards innovation ●●●●●●●●

It is apparent to everyone that #2, #3, and #7 have the most votes.

SCHEDULE	
Introduction, welcome, and purposes	10 minutes
Small groups brainstorm ideas	10 minutes
Small groups agree on their three best ideas	2 minutes
Small groups work together and agree on best ideas	10–15 minutes
Facilitator records ideas in full view	10 minutes
Las Vegas Voting (optional)	5 minutes
Total Time:	**45–60 minutes**

Facilitator Tips:

✓ Starting with groups of three encourages full participation. Small groups are almost always the best way to go.

✓ The first step (Create) allows people to generate ideas without fear of judgment. This usually yields better ideas because participants don't censure themselves.

✓ The second step (Condense) encourages conversation and disciplined thinking and begins to put some reasonable boundaries around what is possible. A tight timeframe keeps people moving toward outcomes rather than becoming bogged down in debate.

✓ The third step (Collaborate) encourages discussion and sharing of ideas; participants must listen to one another and work together to accomplish the task. It also shows that collaboration can happen in a short period of time.

✓ The summary piece of the design (Communicate) gathers all the ideas from the groups of six. Everything is transparent; the facilitator has no agenda. The facilitator's role is to structure a process that meets an intended outcome (a quality list of ideas). Participants experience group collaboration and, almost always, produce a product about which they feel proud.

Las Vegas Voting (see page 191) gives everyone the same number of votes to use as they see fit. No debate bogs down the meeting, and nobody—not even the CEO—can control the outcome. The process is transparent to all.

Interview Design*

Level of Difficulty:	Challenging
Estimated Time:	2–2½ hours
Thinking Styles Utilized:	Analytics, Practicals, Relators, Possibilities

Synopsis:

This meeting design is one of the most powerful and engaging meeting designs available. It will change the way people think about collaborative discussions because it is interactive, focused, interesting, and outcome based all at the same time. It can be utilized with large groups of 50, 75, even 100 participants, and it can be completed in a relatively modest amount of time. It opens participants to new possibilities and creative approaches to organizing and designing future meetings.

It is impressive to see a large group of 100 people working together collaboratively, openly sharing ideas and information and creating prioritized and strategic information in about 2½ hours. The data obtained from the meeting is undeniable because it is collected with everyone's input and in full view.

The design can create a somewhat difficult logistical challenge because a large room will be needed—participants will be moving around quite a bit. It takes planning up front to be successful, but it is well worth the effort.

---

* Dr. Rod Napier, a colleague of ours, is the original creator of this design. Used by permission of NACUBO: Washington, D.C.

Goals:

1. To solicit information from a large number of stakeholders in an effective and efficient manner

2. To prioritize a large amount of information into "chewable chunks" in a transparent manner

3. To increase collaboration and commitment

4. To quickly produce a quality list of ideas

Logistics:

Materials: 10 flip charts, markers, note pads, pens, movable chairs

Space Needs: A very large, comfortable room with lots of wall space

Number of Participants: 10 to 100 (for more than 100 people, you will need two facilitators)

The Activity:

Using 50 participants as the example, arrange the room in pairs of rows facing each other. In our working example, we have five planning questions.

We will use the following five focus questions to show how the design works:

1) If you were talking with a colleague about our company, how would you describe our company?

2) What must senior leadership do to ensure the success of the strategic planning process?

3) What should be the "guiding principles" of this strategic planning process?

4) What are some important questions we need to ask key stakeholders about the company?

5) What advice do you have for members of the Planning Task Force about the planning process we will be involved with?

Facilitator Tip:

> It is important to stagger the questions in Row B so that when you begin the process, participants are not asking the same question of each other.

The following are some examples of strategic questions we have asked. You will see that you can ask almost any question possible, and you will get honest, coherent responses.

1) What is the main reason we are not a stellar company?

2) What are you most proud about this company?

3) How can we further improve company-wide communication?

4) What challenges do you anticipate us needing to deal with effectively over the next five years?

5) What is one piece of advice you would like to give to the president? To the senior leadership team?

6) What company values must we preserve at all costs?

7) What can we do to improve diversity in the company?

8) What is a best practice that you know about that would help us improve as a company?

9) What key issues must we deal with if we are to achieve excellence as a company?

10) What is one thing we must change (e.g., do more of, less of, get rid of) if we are to be successful in the near future (one to three years)?

11) How would you describe the culture of our company?

12) What are some things you enjoy about our company? What don't you enjoy?

13) What about our history helps us as a company? Hinders us? Hurts us?

14) What are our company values that inform and govern our behavior?

Set up participants in two rows. The participants in Row A will start the interview process. They will ask their "partner," the person sitting across from them, their focus questions and record their partner's responses, *unedited,* for two minutes. (It is important to emphasize the unedited part because this is a data-gathering meeting design. You don't want people deciding on their own whether to include a participant's responses or not.)

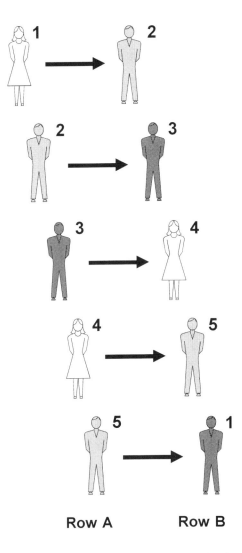

Row A   **Row B**

2. The participants in Row B will then ask their partner their focus question and record their unedited responses for two minutes.

3. After Rows A and B have asked and answered their question, that is the end of a round. People in Row B move down one seat and the person at the end of Row B rotates to the other end of the row.

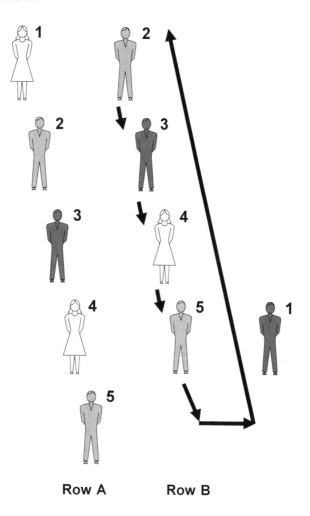

Row A   **Row B**

Facilitator Tip:

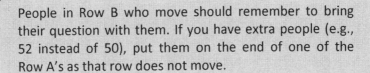

> People in Row B who move should remember to bring their question with them. If you have extra people (e.g., 52 instead of 50), put them on the end of one of the Row A's as that row does not move.

4. After the initial data gathering/interviewing process, have participants sit quietly (10 minutes by themselves) and organize their interview data into one of the following three categories:

   a) **Truths:** These are the responses or answers expressed by almost every person they interviewed. They are very strong ideas—they "leap" off the page.

   b) **Trends:** These are responses given by two or three people. It is not as strong as a "truth," but more than one person provided the answer.

   c) **Unique Ideas:** These are individual ideas that represent a different, creative, unique perspective or idea. It is not a laundry list of every other idea. Each person must judge for themselves if there is a "unique" idea in their interview data that should be part of the database. Once again, participants might find that they do not have a "unique" idea in the interview data.

Facilitator Tip:

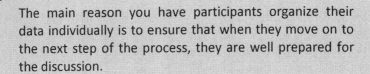

> The main reason you have participants organize their data individually is to ensure that when they move on to the next step of the process, they are well prepared for the discussion.

> Give participants a 15-minute "working" break after the initial interview process because they have been working pretty hard. The emphasis is on "working"; they must do what they need to do to take care of themselves and have their interview data organized into facts, trends, and unique ideas.

5. After individuals have organized their interview data into three categories, have them join with the others who have the same question. In our working model of five questions, you would have five stations with 10 participants at each station.

It is important to remember that when participants are in their question groups that they are now representing the whole group of 50 participants. When they capture the truths, trends, and unique ideas for their question, if one or two group members have a particular idea as a truth, but the other eight participants do not, then the idea is not a truth for the question—rather it is a trend.

6. Instruct participants to use self-managed roles (facilitator, recorder, time keeper, presenter) and take 45 minutes to "pool" their group information regarding their focus question and put the truths, trends, and unique ideas for their focus question on flip chart paper. (For an explanation of these roles, please refer to Self-Managed Groups in the Toolbox section, page 211).

7. After the five focus question groups have created their truths, trends, and unique ideas for their question, have each group present their findings to the larger group. Each presentation should take only three to five minutes.

8. After the presentations, lead a brief discussion about participants' reactions to the shared information (keep the discussion to 10–20 minutes). Once again, let participants know that
their data will be shared with everyone in the room as soon as
possible.

Here are two examples of focus question data for our original five
questions:

What must senior leadership (i.e., the president and SVPs) do to ensure the success of the strategic planning process?

Truths:
- They must be visible and engaged throughout the process.
- They must listen to people.
- They must share all the information we gather with company stakeholders.
- They must be committed to implementing the strategic planning process.

Trends:
- Have regular company meetings to keep people informed about the process.
- The president should include updates about the planning process in his monthly letter to the stakeholders.
- Let us know how the planning decisions will be made.
- Be transparent with the budget.

Unique Ideas:
- Ask the mayor to participate in the planning task force.
- Identify key stakeholders who have expertise in strategic planning and use them as a reality check throughout the process.

What are some important questions we need to ask our key stakeholders about ABC Corporation?

Truths:

- What are the strengths of ABC Corporation? (What do we do well?)
- What are some challenges facing this company over the next 5 to 10 years?
- What two changes/improvements would you make with the physical plant/infrastructure of the company?
- What are the most important trends and issues we need to pay attention to as we plan for the future?
- How would you describe the culture of ABC Corporation (open, welcoming, critical, etc.)?

Trends:

- What are some areas we need to improve as a corporation? (please be specific)
- What is one piece of advice you would like to give to the president that would enable him/her to lead even more effectively?
- What keeps us from being great at everything we do?
- When you talk about ABC Corporation to your family and friends, what do you say?
- How can we further improve corporate communication?

Unique Ideas:

- What difficult issue do we need to openly discuss that currently is avoided?
- How can we further improve collaboration across departments?

SCHEDULE	
Facilitator welcomes participants, explains the purpose of the meeting, and walks through the directions	10–15 minutes
Participants interview each other about the assigned questions	30 minutes
Participants individually organize their interview data into truths, needs, and unique ideas	15 minutes
Groups work with "like" questions, pool their information, and create presentations about their interview data	45 minutes
Groups report their findings	10–15 minutes
Facilitator conducts a brief discussion about people's responses to the overall data	15–20 minutes
Total Time:	**2–2½ hours**

Fish Bowl
Customer/Stakeholder Feedback

Level of Difficulty:	Challenging
Estimated Time:	2–2½ hours
Thinking Styles Utilized:	Practicals, Relators, Possibilities

Synopsis:

Any company needs to be responsive to customers if it is to thrive in a competitive environment. The marketplace is becoming increasingly competitive, and leaders need to be aware of the diverse expectations customers have. The reality is that there are customers or stakeholders everywhere. In addition, today's world has customers and companies linked in ways that tend to have loose boundaries, overlapping needs, and mutually beneficial consequences. The value chain is broader than ever before.

Whether your customers are internal or external, this design can be used to solicit and respond to the explicit and not yet explicit needs of everyone.

Too often, we try to discern the expectations or needs of customers either with a small focus group or with questionnaires, which historically bring a poor return. Both serve a purpose, but this design adds an interesting element by being more interactive and responding to customer/stakeholder feedback in the moment.

In addition, people feel more listened to with this design—it creates the opportunity to build a positive relationship in the future. Participants report that they feel engaged and valued for their input.

The facilitator for this design has to be very good. He or she needs to be able to think quickly, listen carefully, keep things moving, and be good with people. Having an external facilitator is worth the investment.

This design is an adaptation of a Fishbowl activity that has been around for decades. Once again, this could be a meeting between internal service groups, customers and their company representatives, community members, and alumni groups.

Goals:

1. To create the opportunity for constructive discussion of stakeholder concerns

2. To identify the real issues customers have

3. To begin to build positive relationships between employees and customers

Logistics:

Materials: Flip chart paper, easels, markers

Space Needs: A large, comfortable room with movable chairs

Number of Participants: 10 to 20

The Activity:

1. Welcome participants and explain how the meeting will be conducted. Having a handout with pertinent information is helpful. Make sure that all participants understand the process and are comfortable with the proceedings.

2. Have participants introduce themselves and provide any pertinent information (title, department, etc.).

3. In the first Fishbowl, the procurement (P) team sits in the inside circle with the facilitator (F). The focus of this meeting is to deeply understand how the procurement team at XYZ Company perceives the company, to solicit advice on how to improve services, and to establish a real connection with the sales (S) team at XYZ Company.

Stage 1

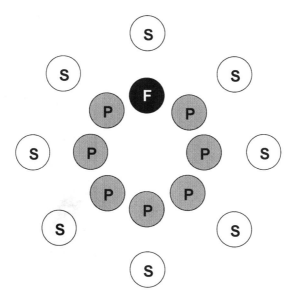

4. Start the discussion with the procurement team by asking the following question: "If you were to describe to a good friend why you worked for this company, what would you say?"

   Make sure that each person in the inner circle has a chance to respond to the question. Allow one to two minutes for each participant, and let them know what the time limit is before starting the discussion. Keep the first round discussion to no more than 20 minutes.

Facilitator Tip:

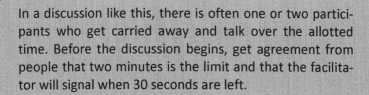

In a discussion like this, there is often one or two participants who get carried away and talk over the allotted time. Before the discussion begins, get agreement from people that two minutes is the limit and that the facilitator will signal when 30 seconds are left.

While you conduct the discussion, the outer circle—the sales team—is listening to the procurement team's response. Encourage them to jot down some notes and capture key points that they are learning from the discussion.

Facilitator Tip:

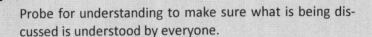

> Probe for understanding to make sure what is being discussed is understood by everyone.

5. The second-round question focuses on seeking advice from the procurement team. Ask participants: "Given your experience here at this company, what is some advice you can give us to further enhance the sales we provide for XYZ Company?"

    Once again, adhere to the one to two minutes per person, keeping the entire discussion to no more than 20 minutes. The sales team (outer circle) is continuing to listen and jot down what they learn.

Facilitator Tip:

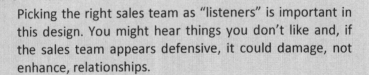

> Picking the right sales team as "listeners" is important in this design. You might hear things you don't like and, if the sales team appears defensive, it could damage, not enhance, relationships.

6. At this time, it might be helpful to take a short 10-minute break to allow people to stretch.

7. After a short break, the sales team then comes into the inner circle while the procurement team sits on the outside.

   The purpose of this round is to glean what the listeners (members of the sales team) heard the procurement team say. Create a sense of openness with the sales team so that they can respond without becoming defensive.

Stage 2

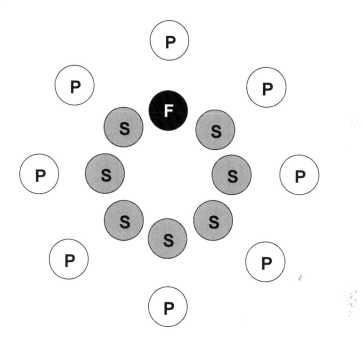

8. This feedback round should last approximately 20 minutes. Some possible questions to focus discussion are:
   - What have you heard?
   - What stands out?
   - What were some discoveries or surprises?
   - What did you like about what you heard?
   - What concerns do you have?

9. As the sales team is discussing what they heard, record the most important points on a flip chart in full view of everyone. Capturing this information helps to structure the conversation, makes the discussion very real, and is a useful record for later.

10. After the sales team has communicated what they heard the procurement team say (20 minutes), have the sales and procurement teams join in a large circle so that everyone can see one another.

Stage 3

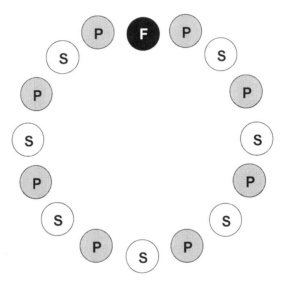

11. Check with the procurement team to see if the sales team captured the essence of their information. Some focus questions could be: "Did we miss anything important?" "Do you feel we heard you?" "Are we on target?" Keep this discussion to about 15 minutes. The primary purpose of this round is to make sure the procurement team felt understood and heard (this almost always happens). This is a reality check more than anything, but a very important step in the process.

12. Have an open discussion that deals with procurement's "advice" to enhance the sales process. Allow the sales team to probe for understanding and clarification nondefensively (e.g., "Bill, you mentioned that the company needs to pay special attention to our planning cycles so that we have the material we need when we need it, am I on target?"). The key is to ensure understanding and clarify any misconceptions (e.g., "Tom, you mentioned we should be able to provide more R&D data to our team in ways they can understand, is that right?"). The goal is to inform, not get caught up in debate or defending what has been happening (e.g., "Tom, it's easy to suggest that we should have customer service 24/7. While we do not have live customer service 24/7, customers are able to access us on the web and receive a response within 24 hours.") **Your primary goal is to seek understanding and right size any misconceptions, not get caught up with negative critiques and debate.**

Allow between 20 and 30 minutes for this discussion. Make sure that things keep moving and people don't get caught defending their ideas.

In the wrap-up, capture any loose ends that may have been created. If the sales team has made a commitment that is a response to advice, that needs to be clarified, and a next step agreed upon. "Mary, you requested a summary of the differences in our 12 products. I believe John said he would get that for you. John, how long will that take?"

Facilitator Tip:

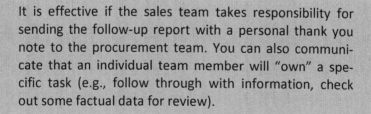

It is effective if the sales team takes responsibility for sending the follow-up report with a personal thank you note to the procurement team. You can also communicate that an individual team member will "own" a specific task (e.g., follow through with information, check out some factual data for review).

SCHEDULE

Facilitator welcomes participants, explains what will take place, and has everyone introduce themselves	15 minutes

First Fishbowl with procurement team
    First question
    Second question
	
	20 minutes
	20 minutes

Break	10 minutes
Sales team comes into the inner circle to share what they heard	20 minutes
Both groups come together to validate what was discussed	15 minutes
Open discussion takes place in which the sales team clarifies and seeks understanding	20–30 minutes
Facilitator has a "wrap-up" discussion to clarify commitments and next steps	10–15 minutes
Facilitator thanks everyone for their participation	2–5 minutes
Total Time:	**2–2½ hours**

Chapter 3
Problem Solving

Not every problem can be solved with just one approach. In this section, we look at a number of innovative approaches to problem solving—some fun and others more challenging—all designed to generate responses and participation from each group member.

Trauma Clinic

In this design, selected stakeholders are brought together to share and solve real organizational problems as a group in a safe environment where mistakes can be openly addressed. The process enables new and different ideas and perspectives to be created, builds the problem-solving capacity of the group, and leaves participants feeling like they've made a real contribution.

Engaged Problem Solving

People seem to have a hard time thinking "out-of-the-box." Engaged Problem Solving focuses on creativity, collaboration, and feedback—three activities that generate high-quality, exciting, and practical solutions.

The Pre-Mortem

We're more familiar with the term *post-mortem* than *pre-mortem*. This design focuses on forward thinking rather than reflecting on the past. It builds strategic thinking and problem-solving skills by anticipating problems before implementing an action plan.

Solutions Matrix

Decisions, decisions: The key to effective planning is the ability to make smart decisions, but that's often challenging in a group setting. The Solutions Matrix helps a planning group effectively prioritize a set of ideas, recommendations, or proposals, lending a sense of objectivity to the decision-making process.

Metaphorical Problem Solving

Metaphors can sometimes capture the essence of an issue or situation in ways that defy simple description. To generate a different and potentially better solution, sometimes a different lens is helpful. In this design, we use metaphors to describe a concern, problem, or challenge. Participants are then asked to "solve the metaphor" and then transfer the metaphorical solutions into real and relevant solutions.

Trauma Clinic

Level of Difficulty:	Challenging
Estimated Time:	2–3½ hours
Thinking Styles Utilized:	Practicals, Relators, Possibilities

Synopsis:

In organizational life and in every industry, there are complex problems to solve every day. During a change process, problems tend to increase in pace, complexity, and quantity. How problems are solved determines the quality of life stakeholders experience and influences the customer experience. In the past, problem solving was seen wholly as senior management's prerogative. That has changed.

Because organizational problems are distributed throughout an organization, senior management can never know enough to deal with all the important issues and challenges. The key is to tap into experience and ideas that are embedded everywhere. The most effective leaders encourage the participation of others in solving problems. They realize that good ideas are everywhere and their responsibility is to organize the opportunity (or "design" it) for employees to come together and work hard on the most critical issues and concerns.

In this design, selected stakeholders are brought together to share and solve real organizational problems. This design could work with executive teams, boards, quality teams, managers, etc. What makes the design work is that it enables new and different ideas and perspectives to be created. It fully engages participants (they work very hard), builds the problem-solving capacity of the group, and usually leaves participants with the feeling they have made a real contribution.

One caution: this design will work only if the climate is safe for sharing real-life organizational problems. If mistakes are not tolerated or talked about, the trust level will be very low. Without some level of healthy trust, the risks are too great for this design to be effective. The leader must be sensitive to the organizational culture and make an intelligent judgment call about this design.

Goals:

1. To engage employees in solving real organizational problems

2. To tap the resources, experiences, and perspectives of all participants

3. To build the problem-solving capacity of stakeholders

4. To begin to develop a diagnostic mentality in all the participants

Logistics:

Materials: Flip chart paper, easels, markers

Space Needs: Large, comfortable room with movable chairs

Number of Participants: 12 to 24 (for this example, 24 participants will be used)

The Activity:

1. Welcome participants and have everyone briefly introduce themselves (e.g., name, role, years at organization).

2. Review the purposes of the meeting (e.g., to solve real organizational problems and issues).

3. Have participants count off from one to four. This will result in four groups of six members each, randomly mixed.

4. Within the smaller groups, invite each group member to discuss a tough organizational problem he or she is currently facing. (**Alternative:** Some group members might want to discuss a problem they have faced in the recent past that wasn't resolved to their satisfaction but on which they would like

some advice or insight). Allow approximately 20 minutes for this part of the design, or about three minutes per problem per person. For example:

- A new team member is just not performing well.
- The communication between two important work groups has broken down.
- An agreed-upon safety protocol is not being followed.
- A formerly good employee is performing poorly.
- Quality control between shifts has a wide variance.
- There is open conflict between sales and production and you don't know what to do.

5. After all participants have shared their organizational problem, give each group two minutes to select one to share with the larger group. This selected problem should be a richly complex one that others will learn from the most and one that is actually "solvable."

6. Have each group share their problem with the larger group. Everyone should hear all four problems.

7. Before the reporting, tell participants, "We are going to act as consultants to one another." Each group will "inherit" one problem from another group and act as consultants to that group.

Here is how it works:

1) Group B acts as a consultant to Group A
2) Group C acts as a consultant to Group B
3) Group D acts as a consultant to Group C
4) Group A acts as a consultant to Group D

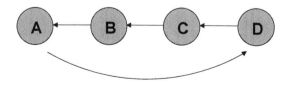

Facilitator Tip:

> One of the key lessons we have learned about problem solving is the value of a different perspective. Often, when people are stuck on a problem, it is because they are too close to it and can't envision alternatives or possibilities. Having someone else inherit the problem creates an opportunity for new ideas and information.

8. After everyone hears all four tough organizational problems (one from each group) and inherits another group's problem, give each consulting group 10 minutes to come up with five or six diagnostic questions that will enable them to better understand their inherited problem. These questions should be worded in a manner that will enable the consulting group to diagnose its inherited problem and to more fully understand the complexity of the other's situation. Have the groups assign a recorder to capture their diagnostic questions. Examples:

    - How long has this problem existed?

    - How has this problem been handled in the past?

    - What would success look like to you?

    - Does senior management understand the impact of this problem (e.g., time, money, opportunity costs)?

9. After each consulting group has had 10 minutes to create their diagnostic questions, give each group the opportunity to ask their questions. Take one problem at a time and have each consulting group ask their questions. It is helpful for all participants to hear the quality of the questions that are being asked.

Facilitator Tip:

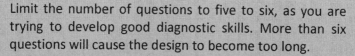

Limit the number of questions to five to six, as you are trying to develop good diagnostic skills. More than six questions will cause the design to become too long.

Caution participants to stay away from "yes" or "no" type questions. Open-ended questions tend to be most helpful with this design (e.g., "What are some things you have already tried to do in solving this problem?" is more effective than "Did you try X?").

As participants ask their questions and receive new information, there will be a tendency to ask follow-up questions. Be fairly strict about this. The purpose of five or six questions is to create quality information. If you give more than the allotted time, this design will begin to drag. Avoid this.

10. At this time, take a 10- to 15-minute break. At this stage of the design, participants have accomplished several things:

   - discussed tough, real-life organizational problems
   - selected one tough problem to solve
   - inherited another group's problem
   - created diagnostic questions to be more fully informed
   - had an opportunity to ask their questions and received new and valuable information

Facilitator Tip:

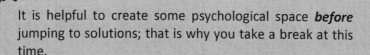

It is helpful to create some psychological space *before* jumping to solutions; that is why you take a break at this time.

11. When participants return from their break, provide each group with the opportunity to ask one "bonus" or follow-up question. Sometimes participants have a new insight they want to explore.

12. Then, once each group has asked their bonus question and has the answer to it, allow each group 15 minutes to come up with ideas on how to solve their consulting problem. Their goal is to act as consultants and provide high-quality, creative, and doable ideas for their client. Once again, suggest that the groups appoint a recorder (a different one this time) to capture the group's consulting ideas.

13. At this time, have each consulting group take a turn sharing their advice and ideas about their client's problem. After the consulting group provides its ideas, open up the floor and ask the larger group if they have any additional advice or insights into the focus problem. Limit this to several minutes and then go on to the next problem.

14. After the final round, open up the floor and have participants discuss their reactions to the design. Keep this to 10 minutes or so. It is usually helpful to hear what people have to say about all the ideas that have been shared. Thank participants and end the meeting. If there have been commitments made (e.g., a participant agrees to meet with someone to discuss strategy about a particular problem or someone agrees to follow-up on something), clarify this and get the participants' agreement before people leave.

Facilitator Tip:

> The key element in this design is to keep things moving. Carefully explain each step, monitor time, make sure participants stick to the rules, and watch out for any wandering off course.

SCHEDULE

Facilitator welcomes participants and people introduce themselves	5–10 minutes
Facilitator reviews purposes of the meeting	5 minutes
Participants count off and reconvene into four mixed groups	2–3 minutes
Participants discuss real-life organizational problems	20 minutes
Small groups come up with the toughest problem to solve and share with large group	3 minutes
Consulting groups create five to six diagnostic questions	10–12 minutes
Consulting groups ask their questions	20–30 minutes
Break	10–15 minutes
Bonus questions	5 minutes
Consulting groups come up with ideas to help solve real problems	15 minutes
Consulting groups share their ideas with their clients.	20–30 minutes
Facilitator has open discussion about participants' reactions and clarifies commitment	10–12 minutes
Total Time:	**2–3½ hours**

Engaged Problem Solving

Level of Difficulty: Moderate

Estimated Time: 2–2½ hours

Thinking Styles Utilized: Practicals, Relators, Possibilities

Synopsis:

If you are engaged in any kind of long-term process and you surface some immediate organizational issues, you will want to address these as soon as possible. This activity enables you to address real issues and come up with quality solutions in a very quick time frame.

What makes this activity engaging is the opportunity to give and receive constructive feedback from fellow meeting participants. The feedback process is done in a way that enhances collaboration and the quality of the final solution.

Too often in organizations, when people are brought together to create solutions to identified problems, the results are less than optimal. People have a hard time thinking out-of-the-box—thinking in different ways—and end up rehashing old ideas. Engaged problem solving encourages creativity, collaboration, and feedback. These three main ingredients ensure that high-quality, exciting, and practical solutions will emerge.

In this activity, it is very important to make sure that the people who will be involved in creating solutions around a particular issue or issues are knowledgeable and competent. Just bringing a diverse group of people together to create some ideas is a waste of time. It is important to be selective and it would be best if they knew ahead of time what the focus of the organizational problems will be. *Thinking about them ahead of time enhances quality.*

The key to the success of this activity is the feedback round. Often when people receive feedback or constructive criticism about suggested ideas or solutions, they become protective of their ideas and reactive to outsiders. To countermand that tendency, the feedback round is designed in a way that creates a level playing field—everyone gets a chance to engage in feedback that is focused on strengthening the ideas instead of tearing down ideas. The quality of solutions are enhanced, and participants get excited and engaged, as well as a real sense of what collaboration is all about.

Goals:

1. To create the opportunity for participants to engage in problem-solving real issues

2. To tap the resources of all participants

3. To provide effective feedback for all solutions in a way that leverages learning and increases the quality of the final product

4. To create more openness and transparency

Logistics:

Materials: Flip chart paper, easels (one for each problem-solving group), markers

Space Needs: Large comfortable room with movable chairs

Number of Participants: 12 to 24 (for this example, 24 participants will be used)

The Activity:

1. Have participants count off from one to six. This will result in six groups of four members each, randomly mixed.

2. After participants are in mixed groups, number each group one through six. It is important that each group has a number and that all participants know the number of their group. Place a large group number on the flip chart next to each group.

3. After each group is numbered, give participants a problem statement to solve. Examples:

   - How do we improve communication technology throughout the organization?

   - What are ways to reduce costs in our operating procedures?

   - How do we get a handle on our inventory?

   - How do we ensure high quality control for our production process?

   - How do we improve our organizational brand?

   - What opportunities in the marketplace should we be taking advantage of?

4. Give each problem-solving group 20 minutes to come up with ideas and solutions to solve their particular problem. A recorder needs to be identified in this round to capture the group's suggestions and ideas.

5. After the problem-solving round, ask each group member, **excluding** the recorder, to count off, one to six. After all participants have an individual number, ask them to go to the group number that corresponds to their individual number (e.g., if I have an individual number of 3, then I go to the group numbered 3). The recorder should remain with his/her original group number.

   The goal is to completely redistribute the participants so that during the feedback round, you have one member from each problem-solving group. This way each group has a diverse set of participants giving feedback.

Facilitator Tip:

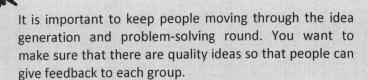

It is important to keep people moving through the idea generation and problem-solving round. You want to make sure that there are quality ideas so that people can give feedback to each group.

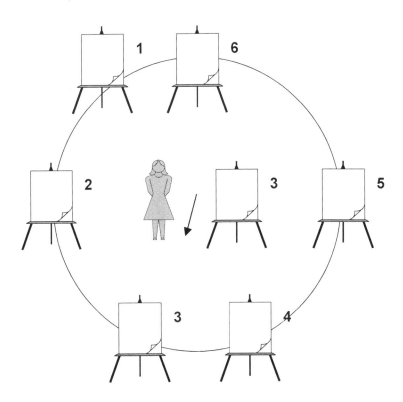

6. The second round is the **feedback** round. The recorder will present the group's ideas and solutions to the new group members. They will listen carefully and provide feedback by sharing with the recorder in each group what they *liked about* the ideas, and the recorder will take notes. Then they will share *advice to improve* the ideas and, once again, the recorder will take notes. Allow about 20 minutes for this segment.

Facilitator Tip:

In the beginning, create a climate that is open to feedback. You need to let people know that this is part of the whole process. The final goal is to listen so that you can further enhance the quality of the work.

7. After the **feedback** round, participants go back to their *original* problem-solving groups. The recorder then shares the feedback they received from the feedback round, and each group has 15 minutes to enhance their original solutions with the feedback received from the other participants. They need to be ready to make a short presentation (no more than 5 minutes) to the larger group. Their ideas should be put on the flip chart for final presentation to the larger group. Allow a total of 30 minutes for all the groups to present their ideas.

SCHEDULE	
Introduction of activity and instructions	10 minutes
Facilitator conducts problem-solving round	30–40 minutes
Facilitator conducts feedback round	20–35 minutes
Original group enhances their ideas after listening to the feedback	30–35 minutes
Each problem-solving group presents ideas (5 minutes/group)	30 minutes
Total Time:	**2–2½ hours**

Alternatives:

1. If you make the groups larger (six in a group instead of four), you will save time on the presentation round because you will have fewer groups to present.

2. You can reduce the feedback round to 10 minutes if you just ask what people liked about the suggested solutions. By reducing the feedback round, you will also save time in the enhancement of the ideas round because participants will have more limited feedback.

The Pre-Mortem

Level of Difficulty: Challenging

Estimated Time: 1½–2 hours

Thinking Styles Utilized: Practicals, Relators, Possibilities

Synopsis:

A post-mortem is used to reflect on what happened after an event (for example, a death, an organizational failure, or a crisis). In contrast, using a pre-mortem before undertaking an action or initiative provides an alternative and useful perspective. First by looking forward, then backward, this design anticipates potential pitfalls, hurdles, and potholes that lie ahead that could prevent successful implementation of recommendations and action plans.

An important strategic question should be asked for any meeting where stakeholders create action plans for implementation: *What could go wrong with this action plan?* People tend to avoid this question, especially when they have worked hard to create the action or implementation plan. They want to create momentum by accomplishing something rather than identifying the challenges to success. Anticipating what could go wrong may seem counterintuitive to success, but it helps build strategic thinking and problem-solving skills as well as enhances implementation.

It is best to use this design a few days after a group has created an implementation or action plan. That gives the group time to digest their ideas and gain psychological distance from their implementation plans. After a few days, group members can be more objective about their ideas and more open to identifying potential challenges. This design also incorporates the highly interactive Carousel Design (refer to Chapter 2) to gather and prioritize the best ideas.

Goals:

1. To identify real hurdles to the successful implementation of ideas/recommendations

2. To develop the problem-solving skills of participants

Logistics:

Materials: Flip chart paper, easels, a magic marker for every participant, masking tape, timers, chimes (or a bell), definitions of terms, Carousel Design handout

Space Needs: Large, comfortable room where participants can move around easily, plus a lot of usable wall space

Number of Participants: 10 to 40 (for this example, 30 participants will be used)

The Activity:

1. Have participants count off from one to six. This will result in groups of five members each, randomly mixed.

   Set up six flip charts as follows:

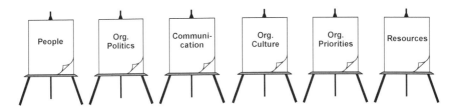

2. Welcome participants and explain the purpose of the meeting: "Today we want to anticipate what could go wrong with our action plans **before** we try to implement them."

3. Communicate the following: "Imagine we are all back here one year from now. Although we have worked long and hard, we have failed to implement our proposed action plans as we expected. We are here today to diagnose what went wrong. We are going to look at six specific elements that blocked our successful implementation. They are:

1) Organizational politics
2) Organizational culture
3) Organizational priorities
4) Resources (technology, money)
5) People
6) Communication

As you work in your groups, please think ahead one year from now and anticipate some of the reasons we were *not* successful. What blocks, challenges, or hurdles can you identify that might have gotten in our way?"

4. Review the definitions of each element (see page 82) and give each group about five minutes to individually record statements that relate to the above elements. For example, for the organizational politics element a statement might be "We should have prepared the Global Regulatory Department to act as advocates for solving this problem."

5. After ensuring that everyone has a marker, instruct the group members to go to the flip chart with the theme corresponding to their number and individually print their answers to the focus question. Participants who agree with someone else's comments should indicate agreement by checking (√) the statement. If they don't agree, they make no mark. (This design is about individual data gathering, not group agreement.) This is another version of the Carousel Design described earlier (see Chapter 2).

6. At the end of five minutes, ring the chimes (or bell) to signal that it is time for each group to move clockwise to the next station. Make sure everyone stays with their group while the rotation occurs. Repeat the process so that each group has five minutes at each station.

    After five minutes, ring the chimes (or bell) and instruct each group to rotate clockwise to the next station. Participants read the information that has already been written down and individually check off all the ideas with which they agree. They also add their own ideas.

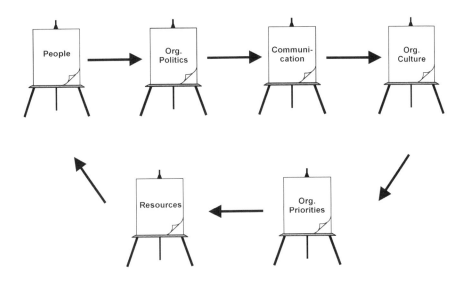

7. The rotations continue until each group has provided individual input for all six elements. This will take about 20 to 30 minutes, but will provide the group with a great deal of strategic information. The output might look like this:

Organizational Politics

We never identified the informal leaders who needed to buy into our implementation plan. ✓✓✓✓

We never got real buy-in from all levels of employees. ✓✓✓✓✓✓

We didn't understand the complexity of the governance process. ✓✓✓✓

The board was not educated about the implications of the strategic plan. ✓✓✓

Competing interests at the executive level stopped any real progress. ✓✓

At this stage, there are two options: You can either assign participants to a strategic element or let them self-select an element of personal interest.

8. Once the groups have formed, explain the task as follows: "In the next 30 minutes, we would like you to come up with some strong recommendations that would effectively deal with the identified challenges for your strategic element. Please use the information we have created to inform your thinking." Use the self-managed roles (refer to Self-Managed Groups in the Toolbox section for descriptions of the roles).

9. Ring the chimes (bell) after 30 minutes and ask each group to present its strong recommendations to the larger group for review and feedback. For example, the Organizational Politics presentation might look like this:

Organizational Politics

We never identified the informal leaders who needed to buy into our implementation plan.

- Identify a list of informal leaders who are essential to helping us succeed with implementing our action plan.
- Invite these informal leaders to a review meeting about our proposed action plan and actively solicit feedback from them. Key leaders should host and facilitate this meeting.
- Ask these leaders how we can best keep them informed about our progress *throughout* the implementation process.
- Provide opportunities throughout the implementation process to solicit their ideas and feedback so that this is not a one-shot deal.

Organizational Politics

We never got real buy-in from all levels of employees.

- The implementation team for the action plan needs to chart the source for an influence plan that is targeted to all levels.
- Each member of the implementation team needs to get educated about the governance process.
- We need to schedule updates about the progress of the action plan at town hall meetings.

10. After the six presentations have concluded, the group decides who will do what. Having a lot of good ideas isn't enough; people must commit to implementing the ideas. Each diagnostic element needs someone to take ownership of the recommendations and move them forward. This does not mean the "owner" must do everything recommended, but should identify key people who could help implement the best ideas.

11. Reconvene the same group two or three weeks later and report the progress of the recommendations. This communicates that some efforts are already successful, builds a sense of accountability that recommended actions will be paid attention to, and develops the strategic notion that anticipating problems before they occur is a smart move.

SCHEDULE

Facilitator welcomes participants, shares purpose, and reviews definition of terms	10 minutes
Facilitator uses a counting-off method to create six randomly mixed groups	5 minutes
The six groups rotate to all stations and write down their individual answers for each diagnostic element	25–30 minutes
Groups self-select the diagnostic element they are most interested in and create recommendations	30 minutes
Each group presents their ideas to the large group	20–25 minutes
Open discussion about who will follow through with the recommendations	15–30 minutes
Total Time:	**1½–2 hours**

BASIC DEFINITIONS

When conducting a pre-mortem, it is helpful to offer definitions of the six elements during the design. You may use these definitions or develop your own so that participants are clear about the information they need to create.

Organizational Politics. This element deals with how decisions are made about *what* gets done in an organization. This is where *who* wants some things accomplished is more important than *what* needs to be done. It also deals with governance processes and what certain groups (such as senior leadership) want or don't want.

Organizational Culture. This involves the organizational norms and values that influence behavior and decision making. It is "the way things get done around here" yet is rarely explicit. Almost everyone clearly understands what gets rewarded and punished in their organization without openly discussing it.

Organizational Priorities. These are the organization's formal and informal goals and objectives. If an action plan is not aligned with where the organization wants to go, it will have many challenges. Problems arise, for example, if the leaders want to accomplish something in contrast to what the CEO thinks is possible or relevant. Friction will likely result if the leaders want to have a national presence and the strategic goals are more regionally focused.

Resources. These can be defined as money, technology, leadership attention, time, and physical space—all the elements that are needed to support an action. It is important to think through what needs to be in place to successfully implement a plan.

People. You must have the appropriate number of people necessary to implement an action plan. For example, if you are creating a new program, a certain number of people are needed to resource it. You also need the right kind of people to implement an action plan. Just having bodies isn't enough—they have to be the right bodies. This element also relates to stakeholders, both internal and external, who can help or hurt the implementation of an action plan.

Communication. Without effective, efficient information sharing, implementation will falter. Communication also has to be transparent and timely. When people don't receive information, they don't feel valued. It is essential to create a variety of communication vehicles (face-to-face, Internet, small- and large-group meetings, newsletters, etc.) that will help keep people informed.

Solutions Matrix

Level of Difficulty: Moderate

Estimated Time: 1–1½ hours

Thinking Styles Utilized: Analytics, Practicals

Synopsis:

When it comes to actually making decisions in planning and change efforts, a group's effectiveness can easily break down. Conflict arises, strong opinions are shared, discussion can become polarized, and the group gets demoralized. Making decisions can be very difficult.

A key to effective planning and change is the ability to have groups consistently make good decisions. Agreeing *ahead of time* on the criteria for the best decision improves both the quality of the decisions and the group process.

The Solutions Matrix will enable a planning group/task force/ team to effectively prioritize a set of ideas, recommendations, or proposals. It lends a sense of objectivity to the decision-making process.

Goals:

1. To prioritize a set of solutions/recommendations
2. To create a transparent and thoughtful process that identifies the best solutions/ideas

Logistics:

Materials: Flip chart paper, easels, and markers

Space Needs: Comfortable room with plenty of usable wall space

Number of Participants: 4 to 8

The Activity:

1. Write the recommendations and proposals on the flip chart so that everyone can see them. Proposed solutions may look like this:

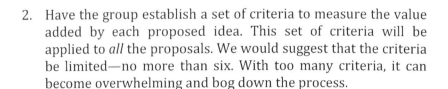

> ### Theme: Improving Customer Service
>
> - Give a 10% rebate check to priority customers
> - Provide two hours of training per week for all customer service representatives
> - Create a one-week training program in customer service for all new employees
> - Pay bonuses to employees that have received positive responses from customers
> - Invest in a new computer tracking system
> - Outsource inventory control
> - Conduct several customer focus groups to determine where we can improve

2. Have the group establish a set of criteria to measure the value added by each proposed idea. This set of criteria will be applied to *all* the proposals. We would suggest that the criteria be limited—no more than six. With too many criteria, it can become overwhelming and bog down the process.

3. After the group has established a set of criteria they are comfortable with, have each member rate the proposals individually, using the established criteria.

4. After each group member has rated the proposals individually, have them share their scores with the group. Someone in the group should act as a recorder and plot the scores on the Solutions Matrix on the flip chart.

The following are the criteria for our example of Improving Customer Service:

Customer Benefit: How much potential customer satisfaction would come from using this solution?

Employee Satisfaction: What is the potential for improving employee satisfaction from using this idea?

Measurable Results: Will the proposal be quantifiable?

Success Potential: Will this proposal be supported by the organization?

Strategic Importance: How important is the solution in achieving the organization's overall strategy?

Cost: How much will this recommendation cost? Is it within the current budget?

A sample Solutions Matrix based on our example is shown on the following page. We used a rating scale of 1 to 5 because we have found it to be the most effective.

In our example, the ***Cost criteria is scored differently*** than the other criteria. If a proposed solution is inexpensive and was within budget, it would get a score of 4 or 5. If a particular solution was very expensive and needed extra resources to fund it, it would get a 1 or 2.

	Customer Benefit	Employee Satisfaction	Measurable Results	Success Potential	Strategic Importance	Cost	Totals
1) 10% Rebates	2, 1, 2, 1	1, 1, 1, 1	2, 1, 3, 3	2, 1, 2, 2	2, 2, 2, 2	1, 1, 2, 1	39
2) Weekly training	3, 2, 2, 3	2, 4, 4, 3	2, 2, 2, 2	2, 4, 2, 4	1, 1, 1, 3	1, 2, 1, 2	55
3) Training week for new employees	4, 2, 3, 4	2, 2, 5, 5	2, 3, 2, 1	3, 3, 3, 3	2, 3, 3, 3	1, 2, 2, 2	65
4) Bonuses to employees	2, 1, 1, 2	5, 5, 5, 5	5, 4, 4, 4	4, 4, 3, 4	3, 3, 3, 3,	1, 2, 2, 1	76
5) Invest in new computer	5, 3, 5, 3	4, 4, 4, 5	3, 4, 4, 3	3, 3, 4, 2	4, 5, 5, 4	1, 1, 1, 1	81
6) Outsource inventory	2, 3, 2, 2	1, 1, 2, 1	3, 4, 3, 3	2, 1, 3, 1	2, 2, 2, 3	2, 1, 1, 2	49
7) Customer focus groups	5, 5, 5, 5	2, 2, 3, 3	4, 3, 5, 3	2, 5, 5, 4	5, 4, 4, 4	4, 3, 3, 4	92

5. After all the scores are plotted, the group can then discuss their reactions to the scores. Focus on any large discrepancies in scores. For example, for the Employee Satisfaction criteria, if you had two group members give it a low score of 2 and two group members give it a 5, the group needs to discuss people's thinking behind the scores. If the group agrees on the criteria ahead of the scoring process, it is rare to see large differences in scores.

In our example, investing in a new computer (81) and having customer focus groups (92) are the top vote getters. The group now has a sense of what the next steps should be, given that all the suggestions had some merit.

If you completed the Solutions Matrix and all the scores are within a few points of each other, the group needs to discuss this. We have found that *avoiding* the number 3 in the scoring can be very helpful in forcing people to choose a higher or lower score. When people aren't sure or want to play it safe, they often give an idea or proposal a 3. Avoid this if you can.

SCHEDULE

Facilitator sets up	5 minutes
Facilitator reviews and posts recommendations	5–10 minutes
Groups establish criteria	20 minutes
Groups discuss rating approach	5 minutes
Each member rates proposals individually	10 minutes
Groups share scores	10–15 minutes
Discussion—reactions, ties, etc.	10–30 minutes
Total Time:	**1–1½ hours**

Metaphorical Problem Solving

Level of Difficulty: Challenging

Estimated Time: 1½ hours

Thinking Styles Utilized: Practicals, Relators, Possibilities

Synopsis:

Metaphors have been around for a long time and are often used to create a powerful image that is easily understood by others. For example:

- "Life is like a bowl of cherries" is one of the classic metaphors.

- "Life is like a box of chocolates" from the movie *Forrest Gump* is a famous metaphor.

- "America is a shining city upon a hill" was used by President Reagan to communicate the power and majesty of America.

- "I have a dream" in Martin Luther King's inspirational and historic speech conveyed the powerful hopes and aspirations of entire generations.

Metaphors can be used to creatively solve problems because they create the psychological space needed to look at a problem in a very different way. They can create a Eureka! moment where you gain insight into how to solve a real problem or organizational challenge (e.g., broken communication process, low morale, quality control issues).

Metaphorical problem solving has three distinct phases:

1. **Create metaphors.** This is where you discover or create a metaphor that describes the problem you are trying to solve.

2. **Solve the metaphor.** This part is what makes metaphorical problem solving so special. You concentrate your energy, thinking, and creativity on trying to solve the metaphor, *not* your real problem.

3. **Transfer your "metaphorical solutions" to your real challenge.** You see if you can apply some of the solutions you created for the metaphor to your real life problem.

Goals:

1. To solve real problems in a creative way
2. To gain insight into complex problems
3. To generate solutions to an identified problem

Logistics:

Materials: Several flip charts and markers

Space Needs: Comfortable rooms with movable chairs

Number of Participants: 8 to 10 people initially, but you can work with 20 to 30 people after you have gained experience with the technique

The Activity:

1. Explain the real organizational problem the group is trying to solve to ensure that everyone is on the same page and clear about the issue.

2. Explain what a metaphor is and give several clear examples (e.g., perfect storm, economic tsunami, toxic assets, troop surge, housing bubble, the dark ages).

Facilitator Tip:

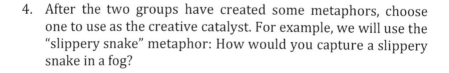

Make sure everyone understands what a metaphor is because you will then ask participants to create metaphors to describe the real problem/challenge.

3. Divide the group of 8 to 10 participants into two different groups and have them generate several metaphors that describe the problem. In our example, we will use "Improving Customer Service" as the challenge. Give the groups 10 minutes to create some metaphors.

    Examples of metaphors for Improving Customer Service might be:

    - This customer service problem is like trying to catch a slippery snake in a fog
    - It's like trying to open a locked box without a key
    - It's like an all terrain vehicle that is headed in the wrong direction

4. After the two groups have created some metaphors, choose one to use as the creative catalyst. For example, we will use the "slippery snake" metaphor: How would you capture a slippery snake in a fog?

Have the group brainstorm solutions to the snake problem. For example:

- Get a flashlight so we can see it.
- Get lots of people involved so it doesn't get away.
- Give it some food so it comes to us.

5. Prioritize the best metaphorical solutions and then have the two groups come up with ways they can transfer the solutions to the real problem. For example:

- Let's hire Jim Seitz who is an expert in this field to spend a day helping us through this. His perspectives are usually very enlightening and his extensive experience will be helpful. (flashlight)

- We just don't have enough brains tackling this problem. We need diverse perspectives throughout the company to help us with it. We are stuck—let's get the right people in the room with us. (people involved)

- We need to create more incentives for our clients so that they come to us more often for our products and services. (food)

- We could utilize deep discounts for frequent users of our products. (food)

- We can pay customers to complete a customer service survey that would provide honest, accurate, and anonymous information about how they view our customer service. (flashlight)

SCHEDULE

Facilitator explains to the group the real organizational problem the group is trying to solve	5 minutes
Facilitator explains the meaning of a metaphor and provides several examples	5 minutes
Facilitator divides the group of 8 to 10 participants into two different groups and has them generate several metaphors that describe the problem; groups choose one metaphor to use as a creative catalyst	20 minutes
Groups then brainstorm solutions based on the metaphor	20 minutes
Facilitator prioritizes the best metaphorical solutions and then has the two groups come up with ways they can transfer the metaphorical solutions to the real problem	30 minutes
Total Time:	**Approximately 1½ hours**

Chapter 4
Sense Making

Some would say that how we make sense of things is the crux of real learning. We all have unique ways of absorbing and integrating information based on our view of the world, our thinking styles, and our learning styles. These exercises will facilitate the development of learning, including new strategies to improve the way they digest and deliver information, introduce some proactive thinking methods that can help achieve future goals, and create broader perspective.

Affinity Diagram

An Affinity Diagram combines both right- and left-brain thinking and is based on the principle that certain ideas can be grouped together because they have an "affinity" for each other. Participants gain a better sense of how ideas are related and uncover hidden connections, leading to more holistic thinking.

Collaborative Teaching Design

This exercise is sometimes referred to as the "jigsaw" because it puts together different elements to form one cohesive piece. It can be used to review multiple reports and articles, and to manage information overload effectively. It creates an integrated synthesis of multiple information elements.

The Future Timeline

Most people and organizations don't take the time to think longer term. The Future Timeline meeting design encourages groups to address events, trends, and issues that could potentially impact their organization over the next 5 to 10 years. It encourages participants to look outward at external realities and, in doing so, strategically plan for future success.

Open Space

It is amazing how much people can learn from each other over a coffee break. Open Space creates a similar opportunity for people to organize their discussions around their individual interests and passions, often generating more beneficial conversation with participants who are fully engaged.

Panel Discussion

Instead of the more traditional panel that addresses a group of listeners, the group members benefit by incorporating panel members into their own smaller groups and interacting with them personally. Focused on a specific issue, the Panel Discussion design is one way participants can become more involved and take ownership of their learning.

Systems Perspective

Did you ever wonder what a coworker's world is really like? What his/her job really entails? It is rare when departments and units get together to share information, but this exercise gives all participants a chance to learn what others in their organization bring to the table, resulting in a unique and useful systems perspective. Having that perspective enables cross-boundary collaboration and problem solving to occur within a more relevant context—a more holistic picture.

 # Affinity Diagram

Level of Difficulty: Easy

Estimated Time: 35–40 minutes

Thinking Styles Utilized: Analytics, Practicals, Possibilities

Synopsis:

An affinity diagram is based on the concept that information or ideas can be grouped together because they have an "affinity" for each other. What makes the affinity diagram so interesting and usable is that it combines right- and left-brain thinking and taps the resources of the group. It allows for the generation of ideas and gives participants a sense of the complexity and interrelatedness of a particular problem.

Further, participants gain perspective in thinking deeply about the hidden connections within a problem or process. The ability to gain a systems view is critical to effective leadership, and this design enables more holistic thinking. Both organic and structural in its development and the final product, it connects to right- and left-brain thinkers.

Goals:

1. To determine the major themes from a large number of ideas, opinions, or issues

2. To enable a group to reach agreement about related ideas

Logistics:

Materials: Flip chart paper, easels, large Post-it® notes, markers

Space Needs: Comfortable room where participants can move about freely with movable chairs

Group Size: 10 to 40 participants

The Activity:

1. Clearly state the problem to be discussed so that participants fully understand the issue. (For example: How do we improve our organizational effectiveness? How do we position our new product in the market? What external threats to our business must we pay attention to?) It is helpful to post the theme on a wall in full view.

2. Generate and record ideas, following the guidelines in Brain-storming (refer to the Toolbox section).

3. Record each idea on large Post-it® notes or strips of flip chart paper.

   Alternative: For larger groups, ask participants to work in pairs to develop their ideas.

4. Randomly lay out completed large Post-it® notes on a wall.

5. After all the ideas have been generated, have participants spend about 10 minutes sorting the cards into related groupings.

    For larger groups (e.g., 40), break the group into three smaller groups. Conduct the sorting process in three rounds:

    Round 1/Group 1: Move ideas into groups in complete silence (4 minutes)

    Round 2/Group 2: Move ideas into groups in complete silence (4 minutes)

    Round 3/Group 3: Move ideas into groups and create categories (headers). This group is able to talk with one another (5 minutes)

Facilitator Tip:

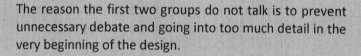

The reason the first two groups do not talk is to prevent unnecessary debate and going into too much detail in the very beginning of the design.

- Make sure that participants work in complete silence with Groups 1 and 2.
- Participants move the cards into groupings simultaneously rather than taking turns.
- Cards can be moved an unlimited number of times.
- It is okay to move more than one card at a time or to merge groups of cards.
- Cards cannot be removed or placed out of reach of the participants.
- One card can be considered a group.

- If disagreements appear to arise (e.g., two people keep moving one card back and forth between two groups), create another card with the same idea and put one in each group.

- The sorting process is complete when people back away from the cards and sorting stops.

6. Now direct participants to label the groupings by writing a "header" card that captures the central theme of the cards within the groupings (see sample diagram below).

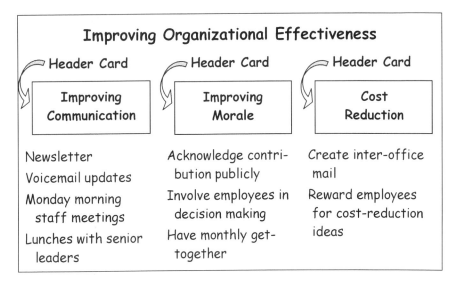

7. Conduct a final review of the groupings to ensure that they make sense and are labeled properly. Final clarification of the meaning of the cards should take place at this time.

8. Transcribe the final affinity diagram onto paper for distribution to participants.

SCHEDULE	
Facilitator states and clarifies the problem	5 minutes
Participants generate ideas while facilitator posts	10–15 minutes
Participants do first sort	5 minutes
Participants do second sort	5 minutes
Participants do third sort and categorize	10 minutes
Total Time:	**30–40 minutes**

Collaborative Teaching Design

Level of Difficulty:	Moderate
Estimated Time:	2–2½ hours
Thinking Styles Utilized:	Analytics, Practicals, Relators, Possibilities

Synopsis:

The Collaborative Teaching Design can be used to review articles, educate participants about key issues, and engage people's thinking. This design is also called the "jigsaw" because it puts together different elements (information). In the end, all the information comes together to provide participants with a coherent and strategic view of what is being considered.

The design carefully manages information overload, leverages participants' time, and gets everyone on the same page in an efficient manner. It has three distinct parts:

- Participants read an assigned document or article and distill meaning from it.

- Participants are placed in mixed groups where all documents or articles are represented to discuss contents, meaning, and implications.

- Participants communicate the essential information distilled from all the information to the large group for discussion.

Goals:

1. To fully involve all participants in reviewing meaningful content
2. To create a body of information that is relevant to participants
3. To connect people and ideas across boundaries

Logistics:

Materials: Reading material for everyone, flip chart paper, easels, markers

Space Needs: Large, comfortable room with movable chairs

Number of Participants: 10 to 50

The Activity:

For this activity, 50 participants and five documents will be used. Create five groups of 10 participants by having people count off from one to five.

Your room should look like this:

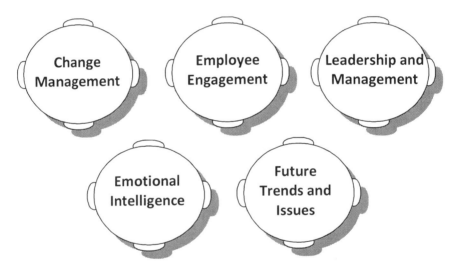

Phase 1:

1. Once people are assigned to their appropriate table, make sure they identify self-managed roles (refer to Self-Managed Groups in the Toolbox section) to help organize their efforts. For this part of the design, each group will need a facilitator and a timekeeper.

2. Instruct each group to read its assigned document or article and generally agree on the top four to six key themes—the ideas that are essential to understand. Although participants can use a flip chart to capture their ideas on paper, also tell them to take notes about the agreed-upon key themes because in the next part of the design, they will share these notes with other participants.

3. Give the groups up to 30 minutes to read their document or article and produce a shared list of the key ideas it contains.

Phase 2:

4. Ask participants to again count off from one to five (because you have five concept documents) and move to the table that corresponds to their new group. This redistributes all the concept document groups to the newly constituted groups, which now have two representatives from each concept document. A reconstituted group should look like this:

Newly Constituted Groups
(Two members from each concept document)

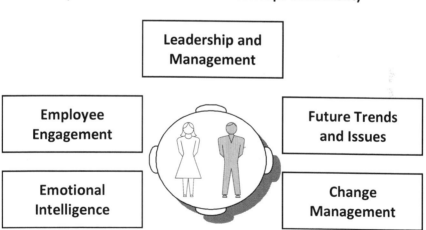

5. The next round brings all the information together into a coherent whole. Once again, ask the groups to identify their self-managed roles before beginning their discussion. For this part of the design, each group will need a facilitator, timekeeper, presenter, and recorder.

6. Let the two people from each concept document who have carried over from the first round share their most important ideas from their earlier discussion (which is why they'll need their notes). Give each pair between 5 to 8 minutes to present their ideas. Then allow several minutes for questions and answers, but everyone should finish sharing ideas about all documents and articles in about 40 minutes.

7. Next, give each group 10 minutes to generate a list of the most critical information from all five content areas. Suggest that they limit this to four, five, or six key ideas, which should be recorded on a flip chart.

Facilitator Tip:

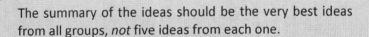

The summary of the ideas should be the very best ideas from all groups, *not* five ideas from each one.

8. **Optional:** Take a 10-minute break at this point because participants have been sitting and thinking for an hour and a half. During the break, organize the flip charts in the front of the room so that presentations can take place immediately after everyone returns.

9. Conclude the Collaborative Teaching Design by asking each group to give a brief presentation on the most important ideas they identified. Because there will be a fair amount of common ground, have each presenter share two key ideas from their group's presentation. This way all groups will have something to share and feel as if their work contributed to the conference. Make as many rounds as necessary to gather all the ideas in the room.

10. After each group has presented, conduct an open discussion with the entire group to bring closure to the design. Limit this discussion to 10 minutes so that people do not go off on conversational tangents. To stimulate the group discussion, ask a provocative question or two. For example:

- As you listened to the key ideas, what resonated most with you?
- Were there any surprises or discoveries?
- What had the most meaning for you personally?
- What is essential to remember?

SCHEDULE	
Participants count off from one to five to divide into five groups and identify self-managed roles	10 minutes
Each group reads assigned document/article and agrees on priority themes	20–30 minutes
Participants count off again from one to five and move to table that corresponds to their new group and identify self-managed roles	10 minutes
Participants present ideas to group—question-and-answer period within the group	40 minutes
Each group generates a list of the most critical information from all five content areas	10 minutes
Break (optional)	10 minutes
Each group gives a brief presentation on the most important ideas identified (limit of 2)	20 minutes
Facilitator conducts an open discussion with the entire group to bring closure to the design	10 minutes
Total Time:	**2–2½ hours**

 # The Future Timeline*

Level of Difficulty:	Moderate
Estimated Time:	1–1¼ hours
Thinking Styles Utilized:	Analytics, Practicals, Relators, Possibilities

Synopsis:

This meeting design enables groups both small (10 people) and large (100+ people) to anticipate the future events, trends, and issues that could potentially impact or influence their organization over the next 5 to 10 years. It is a highly interactive, interesting, and informative design that encourages people to look outward at external realities and create possible future scenarios. Its primary goal is to create a powerful database for strategic planning and thinking.

Goals:

1. To engage participants' thinking about the future and identify priority issues and events that need to be managed effectively if their organization is going to thrive in the future

2. To engage in anticipatory thinking

Logistics:

Materials: Post-it® notes, flip chart paper, magic markers, masking tape

Space Needs: Large, comfortable room with usable wall space (50 feet per timeline)

Number of Participants: 10 to 100

---

* Used by permission of NACUBO: Washington, D.C.

The Activity:

1. Using 48 participants as the example, tape 10 sheets of flip chart paper to the wall—one sheet per year for the next 10 years. (If participants number 100 or more, use two Future Timelines and two facilitators.)

   The room should look like this:

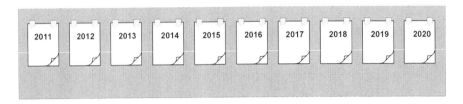

2. Give each participant 10 Post-it® notes.

3. Instruct participants as follows: "Please think about the future events, issues, and trends that could impact or influence— either positively or negatively—the way Incredible Company provides its services, conducts its business, or operates over the next 10 years."

4. Provide several definitions on a flip chart or handout. For example:

   - An event is a single occurrence. (Examples: regulatory legislation, retirement of the CEO, new president)

   - An issue is an important theme with substantial power and influence to impact a company. (Examples: compensation, new product launches, quality issues and recalls, customer service)

   - A trend is an ongoing set of circumstances that has consistency and momentum. (Examples: demographics, aging consumers, increased global competition, slowing economy)

5. After reviewing the definitions and checking for understanding, provide the following instructions:

   - Please write down one event, trend, or issue per Post-it®.

   - Please indicate if a trend or issue will last for a while.

   - Because we will review the Post-it® notes in a few minutes, legibility is important.

   - When you are ready, please go to the Future Timeline and populate it by placing your events, trends, and issues in the years you believe they will occur.

   - If you see a Post-it® note on the timeline that is similar to yours, please check (✓) it to indicate agreement and discard your Post-it®. This reduces redundancies, keeps the Timeline from becoming too cluttered, and captures everyone's information.

6. Give participants about 10 to 12 minutes to think, write on the Post-it® notes, and populate the Future Timeline. This generates a tremendous amount of information for participants to distill and understand.

7. Ask participants to create small, mixed groups of four. Participants can self-organize or use a counting-off method of one to 12, to produce 12 groups of four participants each.

8. Instruct the participants as follows: "Please work with your group of four and review the Post-it® notes on the timeline. Your goal in the next 20 minutes is to search through all the information and generally agree on the three most important issues, events, or trends—not three per category but three in total—that Incredible Company must manage effectively if it is to thrive in the future."

9. After the small groups have reviewed the Future Timeline and agreed on their top three issues, events, and trends, create a master list on flip chart paper in full view of everyone. Using the round-robin approach, take one idea from each group until all the ideas are captured. Check off similar ideas to begin prioritizing the list.

Instruct the group to identify, if they can, a "surprise" or "discovery" from the Post-it® notes. This is when they see an event, trend, or issue they didn't expect to see—sometimes these unanticipated "blips" can become important challenges down the road.

Typically, your master list will contain between 10 and 15 prioritized themes. Your list might look like the one below:

Issues, Events, and Trends

1. There is a dramatic decrease in consumers aged 20-45. ✓✓✓✓✓✓
2. Technology costs will only increase due to the strong demand for cutting-edge technology. ✓✓✓
3. Our dependence on renewals is erratic. ✓✓
4. Our e-commerce capabilities need great improvement. ✓✓✓
5. Our customers are turning toward more technology-based solutions. ✓✓✓✓✓
6. Global competition will greatly increase. ✓✓✓✓✓✓✓✓
7. Competition for the best customers will increase dramatically. ✓✓
8. Many of our leaders will retire over the next decade. ✓✓✓✓✓✓
9. Our president plans to retire in two years. ✓✓✓✓✓✓✓

Surprises and Discoveries

1. Parents of knowledge workers are potential high-end customers.
2. Preparation for leadership is not on the current radar screen.
3. Knowledge workers highly value a sense of place.

SCHEDULE	
Facilitator welcomes participants and explains the purpose and the directions for the design	10 minutes
Participants think about the events, trends, and issues that could impact the institution; write them on Post-it® notes; and populate the Future Timeline	10–12 minutes
Participants self-organize, or the facilitator uses a counting-off method, to place people into working groups of four participants	5 minutes
Small groups review the Future Timeline and generally agree on top-three issues/events/ trends	20 minutes
Small groups also identify a surprise or discovery from the Post-it® notes	5 minutes
Facilitator creates prioritized master list using a round-robin approach	15 minutes
Total Time:	**1–1¼ hours**

Open Space

Level of Difficulty:	Challenging
Estimated Time:	Minimum of 5 hours and up to 3 days
Thinking Styles Utilized:	Analytics, Practicals, Relators, Possibilities

Synopsis:

Open Space was developed by Harrison Owen in 1982. It has been used successfully throughout the world with small groups and with large groups of over 150 people. It can be used in planning processes, organizational redesign, product design, and conferencing. We have found that Open Space is one of the most innovative, interesting, and collaborative processes around. What makes it special is its ability to adapt to any organization's needs. What makes it work is that it creates the opportunity for people to organize their discussions around what they have real interest and passion for.

Open Space was the product of Harrison Owen's frustration with organizing and coordinating an international symposium. Although by traditional standards this symposium was deemed successful, attendees reported that it was the informal meeting times (coffee breaks, early morning and late evening, during mealtimes) that were most beneficial. The reason for this was that it was during these informal times that participants talked about what most interested them. Owen wanted to create an environment where the stimulation and interest shown during the coffee breaks could be extended throughout a conference.

The bottom line is that for Open Space to be effective, it must deal with real business issues that are of passionate concern to those who will be involved. Open Space runs on two fundamentals: passion—without which nobody will be interested—and responsibility—without which nothing will get done. Owen recommends that only volunteers participate in an Open Space meeting.

The requirements of Open Space are few. There must be

1) a clear and compelling theme;
2) an interested and committed group;
3) a time and place; and
4) a leader.

Open Space Technology, A User's Guide, is an outstanding reference for interested parties. Before conducting an Open Space meeting, this book should be required reading.

Goals:

1. To create a powerful meeting

2. To provide the opportunity for participants to talk with each other about what deeply interests them

3. To fully involve all participants

Logistics:

Materials: Flip chart paper, easels, markers, Post-it® notes

Space Needs: Comfortable room where participants can move about freely; comfortable chairs

Number of Participants: 20 to 200

The Activity:

Harrison Owen suggests that five hours is the minimal amount of time for an Open Space meeting, and he usually has two-and-a-half– to three-day meetings. There are four basic stages to an Open Space meeting:

Stage 1: Opening

This should be informal in nature and be conducted by the leader. The leader's role in an Open Space meeting is to help facilitate the meeting's process. The leader cannot have a personal agenda during an Open Space meeting. The leader must have the trust of the group and must give up his/her need for control.

The leader conducts the following activities during the opening:

1. State the theme for the conference; review logistics; and, if participants don't know each other, have them introduce themselves and possibly share something personal with the group.

2. Make sure participants sit in a circle as you conduct the opening. With a large group, you might have to have several concentric circles to accommodate the group.

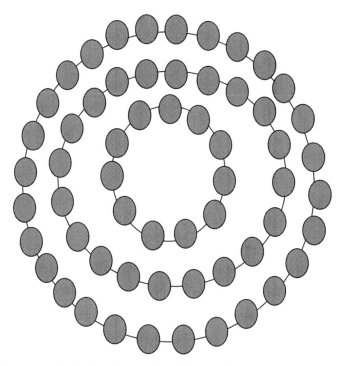

3. Communicate the four *principles* and the one *law* for an Open Space meeting.

   1) **Whoever comes is the right person.** Worrying about who didn't come is distracting.

   2) **Whatever happens is the only thing that could have happened.** Focus on the here and now so that you can recognize opportunities that arise.

3) **Whenever the meeting starts is the right time.** It will operate according to the rhythm of its participants. Buyers buy when they are ready. The creative process does not worry about the clock.

4) **When it's over, it's over.** Selling to disinterested buyers is a waste of time and energy. When buyers stop buying, it's time to move on.

The one *law* of Open Space is the **Law of Two Feet:**

Each participant can and must make a difference in this conference or meeting. If that is not possible in a given situation, then you must use your two feet and move to a new place where you believe you can make a difference. (Owen notes that many people will become "bumblebees," going from meeting to meeting and contributing and learning as they see fit. This is encouraged.)

Stage 2: Creating the Agenda

4. Restate the theme of the conference or meeting and then ask participants, "What are the issues and opportunities for learning what we can talk about today?"

5. Indicate one wall in the room as the Agenda Wall. It is important to remember that the Open Space meeting is designed around people's personal interests and passions. Therefore, the participants create their own agenda.

6. Give the following instructions:

Think about a subject, topic, or idea that you have some real interest in exploring—something that you have a real passion about regarding the conference's theme.

If you choose to, propose or announce a subject for discussion to the entire group, along with your name. An example would be: "My name is Patrick Sanaghan and I would like to talk today about our organizational culture."

After you announce your subject for discussion, you become the convener of that discussion. Go to the middle of the room and put a subject title on a sheet of paper and post it on the designated agenda wall. (When people use one wall to post their subjects, it becomes the agenda wall—see example below.)

Agenda Wall

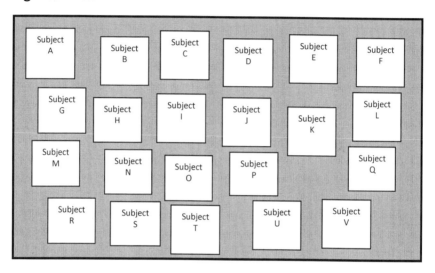

Participants then sign up for the topics they would like to attend. They may sign up for as many as they like.

After you have all had an opportunity to propose a subject for discussion and signed up for the topics you would like to attend, the conveners will move their subject sheets to the Schedule Area (another wall) that indicates places and time slots.

After the conveners have organized the schedule, the Open Space meeting will begin.

Schedule Area

Breakout Rooms	10:00–12:00 Discussion Topic	12:00–2:00 Discussion Topic	2:00–4:00 Discussion Topic	4:00–6:00 Discussion Topic
Room 121	Subject A	Subject B	Subject C	Subject D
Room 125	Subject A	Subject B	Subject C	Subject D
Room 127	Subject A	Subject B	Subject C	Subject D
Room 134	Subject A	Subject B	Subject C	Subject D
Room 136	Subject A	Subject B	Subject C	Subject D
Room 140	Subject A	Subject B	Subject C	Subject D
Room 144	Subject A	Subject B	Subject C	Subject D

Stage 3: The Open Space Meeting

7. Indicate when the schedule is complete and that participants now have the opportunity to go to the breakout rooms and attend the discussions in which they have the most interest.

8. Instruct participants that if there are any announcements to be made or changes in the schedule (extensions, different place, topic, combining groups, etc.) they should put the changes on the flip chart at the easel designated Announcements so that everyone is informed. ***There are no official announcements made during an Open Space meeting.***

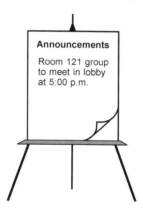

In a longer Open Space meeting of two to three days, you will have several added elements.

• Establish a time for announcements that will be a short period every morning for the group to catch up on what it is doing, where, when, and how. This should be short and sweet. The purpose is to keep people informed, not to hold a discussion.

• Establish "Evening News" as a time for reflection and occasionally fun, but not a formal, report session.

• Schedule a celebration, an opportunity for participants to celebrate that the conference is over. Basic things like food and beverages can be provided, but it does not have to be overly organized. People will do what they're inclined to do, so don't plan this in advance. Just let people know when the time for the celebration will be.

DAY 1	DAY 2	DAY 3
Opening	Announcements	Announcements
Agenda Setting	Open Space	Open Space
Open Space		Closing
Evening News	Evening News	Celebration

Stage 4: Closing

9. Keep the closing simple and serious. This is the opportunity to announce commitments, next steps, and observations about what the event has meant to people. Go back to the original circle or circles and, starting anywhere, allow participants who want the opportunity to say what was important to them about the conference and possibly what they would like to do in the future. (We have used, "What did you learn?" and, "What did it mean to you?" as closing circle stimulus questions). It is important to make clear that no one has to say anything.

10. If the conference requires a formal report, request ahead of time that the conveners of the discussions take responsibility for producing a brief record of what was learned in the discussions. This does not mean that the convener has to write the record; only make sure that someone in the discussion provides a written summary.

    It should be noted that there is no official mealtime during the conference, whether it be five hours or three days. Owen suggests having buffets available so that people can eat when they want. Once again, allow people to do what best meets their needs.

Facilitator Tip:

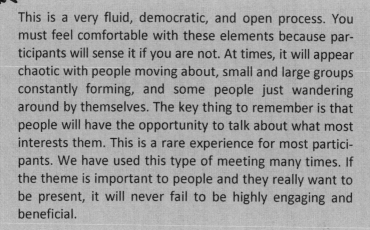

This is a very fluid, democratic, and open process. You must feel comfortable with these elements because participants will sense it if you are not. At times, it will appear chaotic with people moving about, small and large groups constantly forming, and some people just wandering around by themselves. The key thing to remember is that people will have the opportunity to talk about what most interests them. This is a rare experience for most participants. We have used this type of meeting many times. If the theme is important to people and they really want to be present, it will never fail to be highly engaging and beneficial.

Panel Discussion

Level of Difficulty: Moderate

Estimated Time: 1½–3¾ hours

Thinking Styles Utilized: Practicals, Relators, Possibilities

Synopsis:

There is a very different way to conduct a panel discussion and to put "strategic" into people's thinking. All too often, a panel discussion of experts falls flat. The panelists generally sit at a dais in the front of the room taking turns talking to each other or at the participants. Audience members often sit passively and listen to the experts, retaining little and not getting their specific questions answered or concerns addressed. Feedback from the panelists often reflects some disappointment about the experience. This can occur if one particularly charismatic or talkative panelist takes over and leaves the other panelists behind.

This design has both quality control and personal engagement as its core contributions. The result is an opportunity to truly engage the panelists, leverage the learning of all the participants, and allow everyone to reflect on what they have learned. The combination of stimulation and application makes for an inventive design.

The panelists can be individuals within an organization, complete outsiders, or a combination of both. External people on a panel discussion of this type add value. Outside perspectives help prevent a group-think mentality.

The design works best with three to five panelists and between 40 to 50 participants. An adaptation to this design can easily accommodate 100 participants, while still utilizing five panelists.

Goals:

1. To leverage the learning of a group in a powerful manner

2. To personally engage panelists and discover their expertise, opinions, and findings on a subject

3. To engage participants more fully in the learning process and help them take ownership of their learning

Logistics:

Materials: Flip chart paper, easel, markers

Space Needs: Large, comfortable room where participants can move about freely; movable chairs

Number of Participants: 40 to 50 participants and three to five panelists (we will use 40 participants and five panelists as a model for this activity)

The Activity:

1. A critical element of this design is to have a clear central theme that frames the discussion. Tell participants that the panel discussion is for developing strategic ideas for planning, implementation, and/or change initiatives. Tell panelists about the topic areas they will be asked to talk about and their relevance to the participants.

2. Allow the panelists to make some introductory remarks to the 40 participants. The goal is to give participants an idea of each panelist's background, expertise, experience, and perspective. Keep this short, allowing three to five minutes per panelist.

Facilitator Tip:

> Remember that the key to this design is the quality of the panelists. Choose wisely. You want to have people who really know their stuff. They don't have to be charming, just good at what they do.

3. Divide the participants into five equal groups, using a counting-off method or have all the participants in pre-assigned groups. (If you have four panelists, you would create four groups. There should be one group for each panelist.) Each group should then move to designated areas or stations in the room. The room needs to be large enough so that participants can have conversations that don't interfere with each other; if not, breakout rooms will be necessary.

4. After the panelists conclude their introductory remarks, have one panelist join each group.

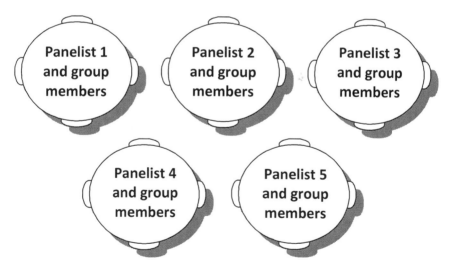

5. Allow each group 10 minutes to ask the questions they want, related to the panelist and his or her area of expertise.

6. After 10 minutes, announce a new round, and have each panelist move to a new group. (Signal when panelists should move in order to keep things on track). You can take a 10-minute break after Round 3 to allow participants and panelists to stretch, hydrate, and take restroom breaks.

Facilitator Tip:

Keep things moving. There is a lot of transition time in this design. Have an agreed-upon process to signal to panelists when to move. You might give a one-minute warning to alert participants. (Using a bell, song, or music with a larger group can work well.)

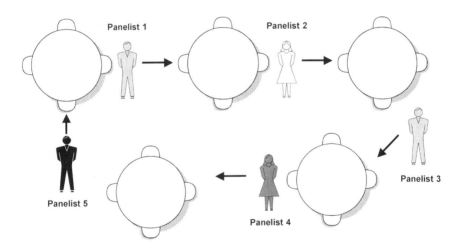

7. Continue this rotation process until each panelist has visited each of the groups once. In this model, the panelist would visit five groups.

8. After the rounds are completed, allow each group 10 to 15 minutes to list on flip charts what they believe were the most important insights they received from listening to the panelists. These most important points should be limited to a maximum of seven or eight and should fit on one flip chart page.

Facilitator Tip:

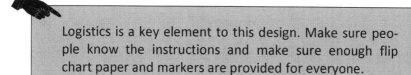

Logistics is a key element to this design. Make sure people know the instructions and make sure enough flip chart paper and markers are provided for everyone.

9. After each group has discussed and written down its most powerful points, have them each give a two-minute presentation about what they have learned to the larger group. The key here is to keep the presentations short and succinct.

10. At the close of the presentations, choose from the following options: have a general discussion with the entire group about their reactions to the panelists' information or their most important learnings. (Allow 15 minutes). Try to distill the common threads that ran through the presentations and capture those on a piece of flip chart paper in order to coalesce the learning. (Allow 15 minutes).

SCHEDULE	
Small groups meet with five panelists for 10 minutes each, allowing 10 minutes of transition time between groups	60 minutes
Small groups list most important learnings for each group	10–15 minutes
Small groups give two-minute presentations to the larger group	10–15 minutes
General discussion of learnings/implications	15 minutes
Total Time:	**1½–2 hours**

See the next page for an alternative to this design.

Alternative:

For a large group of 100 participants and five panelists:

A. After the panelists make their introductory remarks and engage in some limited discussion in front of the large group, divide the large group into five groups of 20 participants each. (***Preassign groups to save time***.)

B. Have groups adjourn to five different breakout rooms. Allow 30 minutes to do the following:

    1) Organize into five small groups of four participants each. Each small group is assigned a panelist and takes 20 minutes to create five to seven of the most engaging questions they can come up with. Their goal with these questions is to engage the panelist's thinking and learn as much as they can from the answers. They are limited to seven questions because they will only have about 20 minutes to ask their questions.

    2) After all the participants have had a chance to create their questions, the panelists then visit each of the breakout rooms. They spend about 20 minutes in each room. They will be going into a room with participants who have already created some stimulating questions for them based on their specific interests.

    3) Panelists will rotate to another room every 20 minutes until they have visited all the breakout rooms. When a new panelist visits a breakout room, the group asks them their prepared questions. There can be time allotted for follow-up questions if the facilitator feels it is helpful. Usually 20-minute segments are long enough to engage and learn from the panelist and short enough to keep participants' interest. (Remember: five panel members × 20 minutes is 1 hour and 40 minutes!)

    After the third round, allow time for an official break.

4) After the break, allow time in each breakout room for participants to list, in their small groups, the most important learning. Have each small group of four report out to the larger breakout group of 20. After all the short presentations have been delivered, the group should assign a volunteer facilitator to distill the most important learning for the breakout group. This might be a short list of five to seven points.

5) Time permitting, have the 100 participants reconvene in the large room and share with each other the most important points from each breakout room. Keep these presentations short. This final activity will bring some sense of closure to the design.

SCHEDULE	
Panelists make introductory remarks	20 minutes
Transitions into the 5 breakout rooms	10 minutes
Small groups create strategic questions for panelists	20 minutes
Panelists visit breakout rooms and answer questions	1 hour and 40 minutes
Break	15 minutes
Small groups reflect on the most important learning and create a short presentation on flip chart paper for the larger group	20 minutes
Each small group makes a 2- to 3-minute presentation to the larger breakout group	15 minutes
Groups reconvene in original room (100 participants and 5 panelists) and hear presentations of the most important learning from each breakout group	20 minutes
Total Time:	**3¾ hours**

Systems Perspective

Level of Difficulty: Moderate to Challenging

Estimated Time: 1½ hours

Thinking Styles Utilized: Analytics, Practicals, Relators, Possibilities

Synopsis:

In most organizations, it is rare that individuals from different work groups or business units get together intentionally to plan, strategize, or collaborate. If this does happen, it usually occurs among the top people in the organization.

This activity enables participants to see the whole picture as a part of planning for the future. This activity could be part of a benchmarking meeting to determine where people are and where they are going, to look for alignment, to determine redundancies, and to problem solve for the future. It can also be the background or springboard for an organization's needs to plan effectively for the future. It gives all participants a unique systems perspective of the organization. Often it is the first time participants have a clear picture of what others in the organization are working on and how they can contribute to the overall effectiveness of the organization. It never fails to be enlightening.

Goals:

1. To share information from different parts of the organization about strategic themes

2. To distill meaning from the shared information

3. To make recommendations for the organization based on real data

Logistics:

Materials: Large blank wall, flip chart paper, markers

Space Needs: Comfortable room where participants can move about freely; comfortable chairs

Number of Participants: At least five individuals from each business unit or work group should attend this meeting. Make sure that the people who come to this work session are knowledgeable and represent the diversity of the business unit or work group (we will use 20 participants from four different business units as a model for this activity).

The Activity:

In a product-oriented company, like the one we will use in our example, we might have finance, customer service, technology, and human resources represented. Each business unit might send a vice president, two general managers, a front line supervisor, and an employee.

Participants should be informed ahead of time that the goal of the meeting will be to share information with other work groups in the organization and to work together to leverage resources and learning. They should know that they will be able to see what other work units are doing throughout the organization and see how they can build on each other's strengths and create productive opportunities for the upcoming year.

Have a grid (like the one shown on the following pages) prepared ahead of time, using butcher or flip chart paper. The grid must be large enough to contain all the information generated and to be seen at a distance of 10' to 15'. It usually takes up an entire wall. Allow for each category to be approximately 3' × 3' square, so that an organization that has six different units participating and five categories would need a grid approximately 18' to 20' long and 10' wide.

SAMPLE GRID				
Categories/Strategic Questions	Customer Service	Technology Department	Human Resources Department	Financial Department
Beliefs/Values				
Four Greatest Strengths of Your Unit				
Three Top Priorities or Challenges in the Next Year				

SAMPLE GRID (concluded)					
Categories/Strategic Questions	Customer Service	Technology Department	Human Resources Department	Financial Department	
Two Areas of Needed Improvement					
One Resource Willing to Share					

1. Ask people to get into their work units (Customer Service, Technology, Finance, etc.). Give them 20 minutes to generate the information to complete the grid.

2. Ask individuals to go up to the grid and fill in the information for their work unit. Allow 15 minutes.

3. After the information has been generated, have one person from each work group do a brief presentation of the written information so that everyone in the room clearly understands what is on the grid or chart. Allow some time for clarification and questions. (See the sample completed grid on pages 138–140).

4. After each group has presented its information, have participants get into mixed groups (one person from each business unit) and diagnose what they have heard and seen. Some possible focus questions might be:

   - What stands out to us? What gets our attention?

   - What are some ways we can leverage our resources?

   - How can we help other business units?

   - What do we need to keep in mind as we plan for the future?

   - Are there challenges we face that are similar? How do we use our collective strengths to manage the challenges?

SAMPLE GRID

Categories/Strategic Questions	Customer Service	Technology Department	Human Resources Department	Financial Department
Beliefs/Values	• People are important • We take pride in the quality of our work • Service attitude • Professionalism is important	• Innovation and creativity are valued • We participate in decisions about technology • Keeping on the "cutting edge" is vital to our success	• People are our greatest asset • Our job is to make employees feel valued	• Quality data is vital in making effective decisions • Our support is key to the success of the organization • Financial information must be understandable to employees
Four Greatest Strengths of Your Unit	• Our people work well together • We are committed to the company's success • Hard-working employees • Knowledge (we know product line)	• Ability to respond to changing demands • Our people keep up with new developments • We are practical when interfacing with others • Creative thinking	• Responsive to employees' needs and requests • Training department receives outstanding grades/feedback • Our people care about employees	• Knowledge of finance • Use of technology • Critical thinking • Integrity of our people

SAMPLE GRID (continued)

Categories/Strategic Questions	Customer Service	Technology Department	Human Resources Department	Financial Department
Three Top Priorities or Challenges in the Next Year	• Building a new program for tracking high-yield customers • Expanding our office space to accommodate new employees • Tightening up our billing procedures	• Building our internal technology capacity • Recruiting excellent technology employees	• Increasing our training program • Negotiating better fees for our medical benefits program • Diversity training	• Electronic budgeting • Training employees about financial realities • Maintaining compliance with new federal regulations
Two Areas of Needed Improvement	• Need to better plan for growth and increasing demand • Need to define "quality" customer service and its cost to organization	• Better communication with our internal stakeholders • Lack of planning	• Need to develop more expertise in planning within our department and throughout the organization	• Tracking internal expenses better • Communicating to all employees about financial realities

139

SAMPLE GRID (concluded)				
Categories/Strategic Questions	Customer Service	Technology Department	Human Resources Department	Financial Department
One Resource Willing to Share	• Our telephone directory systems	• Computer expertise and training for all employees	• Stress and time management training	• We have developed a course on the basis of finance and accounting for "lay" people

5. Have each group also make two or three strong recommendations that the organization should seriously consider. It is important to remember that this group, because of its diversity and knowledge, is in a unique position to see what the organization needs to do because they are seeing the whole picture. Some examples of strong recommendations include the following:

- Our people are our most important asset in each business unit. Because the quality of our people is so high, we must be careful to have only the best candidates for each position.

- Planning seems to be a concern. We need to quickly develop the internal capacity to plan effectively. We may need to hire outside consultants to help us do this.

- We are growing as a company. We need to manage this effectively and keep everyone informed.

- We need to continually get better at what we do (e.g., tracking our best customers, building internal capacity, training employees). Everyone in the organization needs to understand this ongoing drive toward excellence.

- Training is critical to our business. We need to coordinate these efforts so that we don't overwhelm people. The human resources department should coordinate these activities and evaluate their effectiveness.

SCHEDULE

Participants generate information for the strategic themes	20 minutes
Participants fill in the grid with their information	15 minutes
Individuals from each work unit make short (3–5 minute) presentations to the whole group to ensure understanding	20 minutes
Facilitator allows time for clarification and questions regarding information presented	10 minutes
Mixed groups diagnose what they have *seen* and *heard* in the presentations and on the systems information on the wall and make two to three recommendations	30 minutes
Total Time:	**1½ hours**

Facilitator Tip:

The key to the success of this design is to have the right categories and therefore the right information. You want to be able to give people a rich database that they normally don't have access to. Therefore, it is critical to have the strategic areas that you will want to examine well defined. The key to creating an effective question or category is to ask yourself, "What is it that we need to know about our business in order to be better at what we do?" You can ask for different responses when setting up the grid, but try to limit it to no more than six or it will become overwhelming. Some examples that we have used in the past include the following:

- three accomplishments you are most proud of in the past year
- three external threats that make you nervous about the future
- a lost opportunity that your unit wished they had taken advantage of
- three innovative work practices you have been successful with in the past year
- support you need from other work groups
- how you would like others in the organization to use your services

Alternatives:

If you know the categories that are going to be discussed ahead of time, you can request that participants send the completed information before the meeting begins. This way, when people enter the room to do their work, all the relevant information is already on the grid. You should also reproduce this information as a handout for participants. You will need to have short presentations from each business unit to explain the information before you ask people to work in cross-sectional groups to distill information from the grid. This will save approximately 30 minutes.

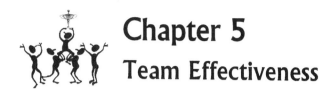

Chapter 5
Team Effectiveness

Team effectiveness is much more than learning to get along. When dealing with a team of people, many of whom think and react differently, enabling the team to achieve more than they would individually is a key to success. These exercises help groups and their leaders learn to work together more effectively by continually communicating and setting clear expectations, then following through—even as the team dynamic changes.

The Team "Talent Audit"

The more team members know about each other individually, the more effective they will be as a whole. The talent audit assesses a team's talents, skills, and qualities so that the team can tap into its resources and utilize them to become more effective. It also increases awareness, collaboration, and commitment to develop and grow.

Team Ground Rules

Ground rules help a team decide as a group what will be expected of each other regarding behavior, meeting management, and other operations. Teams that are in alignment are more successful and likely to avoid potential problems. Ground rules should be incorporated regularly to keep teams on track and are most effective when the team is first formed or a new member joins. This exercise generates vibrant discussion about what is important to a particular team, enabling them to come to a conclusion about the five to six operating principles or norms that really make a difference.

Team Transition Design

It is tough being the "new kid on the block." This design helps new people transition smoothly into a group and also helps glean key information from department group members. With open and direct communication, new team members get on board and contribute much faster.

Creating Group Connections

When change occurs, groups can be thrown together to work on a common project—but they do not always work cohesively. With the help of an outside facilitator, this exercise helps get groups off to a good start by showing them how to address differences and work effectively as a team.

New Leader Assimilation

The first 30 days of new leadership are especially critical, and this process helps new leaders assimilate through open communication in which the group exchanges views, makes recommendations, and clarifies expectations. Leaders have the unique opportunity to learn about areas of concern firsthand, and team members also benefit from the development of shared perspectives.

Team Effectiveness Check-In Discussion

Teams are commonplace in the workforce, but they don't always check in with each other and maintain good communication. This tool encourages proactive communication and unearths implicit points of view, enabling any team to more effectively evolve with change. Finding ways to address issues and differences before they become problems is the sign of a healthy team, and the Team Effectiveness Check-In Discussion is an easy way to do this.

Special Note:

For those individuals who are interested in assessing their own team's effectiveness, HRD Press has published *The Exceptional Team Survey* (2008) written by Patrick Sanaghan, Larry Goldstein, and Andi Trump.

The Team "Talent Audit"

Level of Difficulty:	Easy
Estimated Time:	1 hour
Thinking Styles Utilized:	Analytics, Practicals, Relators, Possibilities

Synopsis:

The purpose of the Talent Audit is to create a robust database of a team's skills, talents, and qualities. It will provide team members and the team leader with the information they need to build a great team.

Although this activity is best utilized with newly formed teams, it can be used anywhere in a team's development with positive results. The more information and insight team members have about each other, the more choice points they have about using the information to leverage team effectiveness.

Goals:

1. Understand the talent on the team
2. Tap the resources of the group
3. Create learning opportunities for each other
4. Begin a discussion about how effective teams actually work

Logistics:

Materials: Flip chart paper, markers

Space Needs: Large room with plenty of wall space

Number of Participants: 8 to 10

The Activity:

1. Allow team members 10 minutes to answer the focus questions and post them on a flip chart in full view of all team members. Each team member then makes a brief presentation (two minutes max) about their information and answers any questions team members might have.

2. We suggest you limit the "audit" to six or seven questions or there will be too much information to meaningfully digest and utilize. We will suggest six questions that work very well in creating the initial database. We will also suggest other questions for your consideration.

   The Classic Six Questions:

   1) **What five strengths do you bring to the table?** (e.g., work ethic; flexibility in thinking; creative problem-solving, ability to deal with conflict) Please stay away from qualities like "honesty" and "integrity." It is assumed that all people have these and we want to understand other "gifts" you bring that will help us achieve stellar results.

   2) **What is something you would like to learn about or a skill you would like to develop?** (e.g., get better at problem solving; improve my decision making; learn how to execute better; use technology more effectively)

   3) **What is one area of needed development you are working on?** (e.g., being more decisive; being less critical; learning how to delegate; managing conflict better; being open to the ideas of others; being a better listener; not getting caught in the weeds when thinking through something)

   4) **What is your preferred learning style?** (e.g., HBDI, linear thinker; theoretical; creative) **or leadership style**? (e.g., MBTI, DISC) (All team members would have to understand the different assessments.)

5) **In your experience, what are the two essential elements of an effective team?** (e.g., respect for each other; ability to listen well; clear purposes and goals; ability to deal with conflict; diversity of ideas; perspective and experience; effective leadership; fairness; keeping commitments)

6) **What are two things we need to know about you in order to work with you most effectively**? (e.g., I come prepared for discussions at meetings; I like to know what the outcomes are; I appreciate regular feedback; I prefer when people are straight and honest with me; I am creative—not flaky; I tend to think in terms of black and white, either/or; I am an excellent planner, please use my skills; I tend to be critical but don't want to hurt people's feelings)

Other potential questions that are helpful include:

- Who is a leader you admire and what qualities did they/do they possess that you find attractive?

- What is a book or article you have read about leadership that influenced who you are?

- What is a "ground rule" or working agreement that you have seen used effectively to enhance team performance?

- What is one thing you would like to change/enhance/get rid of on this team and why? (This question needs to be asked for an ongoing team, not a new one.)

3. The final steps in the audit meeting are to put team members into pairs (or threes) and do some "sense making" about the database that has been created. Have the pairs (or threes) review all the flip charts and ask them to diagnose the information and create a brief report that tells the "story" of the talent in the group.

It is helpful to provide one or two examples. Some suggestions include the following:

- It seems like we have a lot of team members who are linear thinkers (or creative ones).

- There are a few opportunities for leveraging the group's talent by connecting what people would like to learn to some of the strengths others have.

- A lot of us have difficulty managing conflict—we might need training in this.

- Given the task and purposes of the team, we seem to have the talent and skills to be successful.

- Most of us agree that keeping commitments to others is important. Could this be a ground rule we adopt?

Do not over think this part of the activity. The purpose is to have team members dig a little into the rich database they have created. Even if there is some redundancy in the reports, that is fine.

4. Give the pairs (or threes) 10 minutes to review the information and then have each set of team members report their findings to the larger group. You might then consider having a brief, open discussion about team members' reactions to the information that was created. Capture the data in electronic form and distribute to participants as soon as possible.

SCHEDULE

Team members take 10 minutes to answer the focus questions and post them on a flip chart in full view of all team members	10 minutes
Each team member makes a brief presentation on their information and answers any questions others may have	20 minutes
Facilitator puts team members into pairs (or threes) and does some "sense making" about the database that has been created. Pairs review the information on the flip charts and create a brief report that tells the "story" of the talent of the group	20 minutes
Facilitator conducts a brief, open discussion about team members' reactions to the information that was created	10 minutes
Total Time:	**1 hour**

 # Team Ground Rules

Level of Difficulty: Easy

Estimated Time: 1½ hours

Thinking Styles Utilized: Practicals, Relators

Synopsis:

High-performing teams operate with a set of explicit and implicit ground rules. Effectively aligning a team's interactions and behaviors is fundamental to the successful operation of a team. Ground rules help a team decide as a group what they will expect of each other from the standpoint of behavior, meeting management, and other operational team agreements. The key to effective ground rules is to make team members' expectations for each other explicit.

The best time to use this approach is when

- a team first begins working together and
- a new team member or leader joins the team.

This is not a one-time exercise. Ground rules should be incorporated into how the team works together. As an active team, ground rules can be used to help get the team back on track without having to "get personal" by pointing out individual behavior.

Goals:

1. To enable a group to develop a set of operating norms or ground rules
2. To create a focus of what leadership behavior is desired
3. To keep a team from going "off track" over time

Logistics:

Materials: Flip chart paper, easels, markers, tape, index cards or Post-it® notes

Space Needs: Comfortable room

Number of Participants: 6 to 12

The Activity:

1. Explain to the group that having a set of agreed-upon ground rules governing individual behavior facilitates the work of the group and enables the group to be highly effective and productive.

2. Give five index cards or large Post-it® notes and a pen to each person in the group.

3. Ask each person to reflect on and record behaviors they consider ideal behaviors for this group or team. Sometimes it is effective to ask the group to think about a "dream team" they have been a part of—asking them to use that experience to visualize and feel that experience can help them identify what really matters to them in terms of positive team experiences. After that, each team member should record one idea on each of their cards or notes and then hand them to the facilitator.

4. Shuffle all the cards together, then turn the cards face up and read each card aloud, allowing time for the group or team members to discuss each idea. As each card or note is read and discussed briefly, tape each card or note to a flip chart or wall so that all group members can see it. As each subsequent card is read aloud, ask the group to determine if it is similar to another idea that has already been expressed. Cards with similar ideas should be grouped together. (Please refer to the Affinity Diagram located in Chapter 4: Sense Making.)

    An example is shown on the following page.

Communications	Accountability
• Transparent • Honest • No secrets • Timely • Respectful disagreement is encouraged	• Goals are clear to everyone on the team • We hold each other accountable for our commitments • Consequences for not doing what we said we would

Decision Making	Culture
• Seek team input before deciding • We don't have to be perfect • Avoid analysis paralysis • Once a decision is made, get full support by others • Use good data when possible	• Honesty • Be supportive of others • Have some fun • No personal attacks • No triangulation • Trust is essential

5. When all of the cards have been sorted into groups, lead the group in writing the ground rule suggested by that group of cards. The new ground rules should be written on a flip chart.

Agreed-Upon Ground Rules

- No triangulation—be straight with each other
- No secrets—everyone has access to all relevant information
- Support decisions after input is solicited
- Deal with conflict ASAP
- Respectful disagreement is valued
- Have some fun

6. Often the exercise evolves so that the number of ground rules is about four to six. Any more than that can present an overwhelming challenge. The idea of ground rules is that the group or team "flushes out" those that really matter. If there is a problem with too many ground rules, use the Las Vegas Voting technique (refer to the Toolbox section) to come up with the final list.

SCHEDULE	
Facilitator welcomes participants; explains purposes of the meeting	10 minutes
Facilitator distributes index cards to each participant and asks them to write one idea per card	10 minutes
Facilitator shuffles cards and reads each one aloud, then tacks the card onto a flip chart grouping like ideas	20–30 minutes
Facilitator asks group to write ground rules based on the grouping—one team member records new ground rules onto a flip chart	20 minutes
Facilitator reviews the new ground rules with the group and has them reach consensus before adopting	25 minutes
Total Time:	**Approximately 1½ hours**

 # Team Transition Design

Level of Difficulty:	Moderate
Estimated Time:	1–1¼ hours
Thinking Styles Utilized:	Practicals, Relators

Synopsis:

In any long-term change process of six months or more, such as organizational redesign, technology implementation, or strategic planning process, many work groups and teams are created to carry out important work. Due to unforeseen circumstances, some members have to leave the team. In other situations, new members are added because the size and complexity of the change process dictates more support.

The challenge for the team leader is to leverage the opportunity to learn from the departing members and to make new members feel at home with an ongoing group. In fact, you not only want new members to feel welcome, you also need them to make value-added contributions as soon as possible.

You want to avoid the "new kid on the block" syndrome that exists when new members join an intact group. Too often, the new members spend an inordinate amount of time trying to figure out what the norms of the group are. New members often try to be collegial and listen much more than is necessary. They are reluctant to make suggestions. The collaborative leader needs to be able to create the opportunity for new members to contribute fully and not wait until it is "appropriate" to do so. Furthermore, there is much to learn from the veterans who are leaving. This design enables you to get people on board quickly and distill wisdom from those who are leaving.

Norms are powerful influences in any group. The problem with norms is that they are rarely explicit or acknowledged publicly. These unspoken agreements about "how business is done here" need to be made public so that new members can learn as quickly as possible what's expected and appropriate. This design allows you to surface these implicit norms and creates an atmosphere of openness and understanding. What makes it work is its ability to create the opportunity for everyone to teach and learn from each other.

This design has an adaptation, and we will start with the simplest one first.

Goals:
1. To tap the wisdom and experience of veteran team members
2. To discover what new team members can contribute to the team's overall effectiveness

Logistics:

Materials: Paper and pens

Space Needs: Comfortable room with movable chairs

Number of Participants: 5 to 15 people (we will use 10 as a model for this activity)

The Activity:
1. Ask the group of 10 to form two groups. One with veteran members only, the other with the new members. Let participants know that the main purpose of this activity is to have people get to know one another.

Facilitator Tip:

It is important that as the leader you sit with the new members. This will balance the power in the group, create a sense of safety and give the new members permission to be open.

Leader

Veteran Group　　　　**New Group**

2. Have each group come up with five or six questions they would like to ask the members of the other group. Strongly suggest that these questions be crafted so that they allow each group to learn as much as possible from the other group. Some examples new group members might ask include the following:

- What are two or three successes your team has experienced that you are most proud of?

- What are three norms in your group that we should be aware of?

- What are some challenges in being a part of this group and what have you learned from these challenges?

- What do you like most about being a part of this team?

Veterans might ask the following:

- Please describe a time when things didn't go well for you and what you learned from this.
- What are two skills or talents you bring to the table?
- How would you describe your effectiveness as a team player?
- How would a good friend describe you?
- How would someone you have had some difficulties with describe you?

The goal is to ask those questions that rarely get asked. People will often manage the appropriate level of risk regarding what kinds of questions are asked. Double check the questions before participants begin asking them to ensure quality and help manage the risk level.

3. After the two groups have created their five or six questions, suggest that the new members ask their first question. This creates a more level playing field and gives them permission to ask their question. After the veterans have answered the new members' first question, have them ask their first question and listen to the response. This process continues with each group taking a turn asking and answering a question until all questions have been asked.

Facilitator Tip:

As the leader in this design, you need to manage the conversation carefully. Your goals are to keep participants on task, make sure things don't drag on too long, and check for understanding as the process evolves. If you think one of the participants or groups might not have given a complete answer, or that there is some confusion, you can check to see if the other group is getting the information it needs.

4. After all the questions have been answered, conduct a short discussion about participants' reactions to the meeting. It is helpful to hear how participants experienced this activity. It is not necessary to get too deep with this discussion—keep it to 15–20 minutes. It helps create a sense of closure for the group. Some focus questions you might ask to stimulate discussion include the following:

    - What were some discoveries for people? Surprises?

    - What should we keep in mind as we work together in the future?

    - How can we take what we have learned about each other to help us achieve our mission?

SCHEDULE FOR ORIGINAL DESIGN	
Facilitator welcomes participants, explains purposes of the meeting and creates two groups	10 minutes
Each group creates questions for the other group	15 minutes
Each group takes a turn asking and answering questions	20–30 minutes
Facilitator leads a discussion about participants' reactions to question and answer round	15–20 minutes
Total Time:	**1–1¼ hours**

Adaptation of the Design:

Within an intact group where some members are leaving, the following process could be utilized.

1. Have the group members divide into two groups—those who are leaving and those who are staying.

Leaving   **Staying**

2. Provide questions for the departing members and give them 15 minutes to organize their thinking and answers. Some examples include the following:

    • As you look back over this team's work together, what are two or three successes this team had?

    • What are some things this team could have done differently?

    • What personal regrets do you have about this team's work together?

    • What advice or wise counsel can you give to the remaining team members?

    • What is the most important lesson you are leaving with from working with this group?

    • What hopes or wishes do you have for the remaining team members?

The goal is to tap the wisdom and experience of the leaving members. We have found that when people are leaving, it creates the opportunity for real openness. Most importantly, this design asks for their wise counsel and provides the remaining members with quality information they can use to leverage the team's effectiveness in the future. It also honors the contribution of the parting members, which should be valued in every organization.

3. While the departing members are creating the answers to the focus questions, the leader should ask the remaining members to do the following task (give them 15 minutes to do this): "Please list three to five positive contributions of each member who is leaving." The goal is to create the opportunity for each departing member to hear what contributions they made to the team. It is important to be as specific and clear as possible with these contributions. You want to avoid things like: "You are really a nice person." Some examples include the following:

    - "Joy, your organization skills were very helpful. The agendas you provided for our meetings were great."

    - "Lisa, your ability to listen will be missed. There were many times when we experienced difficulties, but your listening to both sides allowed us to move forward."

    - "Chris, your positive energy and can-do attitude was refreshing. You took on the technology project with enthusiasm and professionalism."

    - "Rasheed, your follow-through on assignments was outstanding. You completed every assignment on time."

Facilitator Tip:

> This design adaptation is a judgment call on the part of the facilitator. If a group is impersonal or poorly functioning, this design obviously will not work. You also have to take into account the organizational culture, so choose wisely. Our experience has been that this is a very positive experience for participants. It is rare for people to hear what their contributions have been. Creating the opportunity for team members to hear the wisdom of the leaving members leverages their learning in constructive ways. Everyone is a winner.

4. Follow the basic formula described in the original design. Have the leaving members give the response to one of their questions. Then have the remaining members give one departing member feedback on their positive contribution. Follow this process until all the questions have been asked and the leaving members have heard about their positive contributions.

SCHEDULE FOR ADAPTATION

Facilitator welcomes participants, explains purposes of the meeting, and creates two groups: departing and remaining members	10 minutes
Both groups work on their assigned tasks (advice and contributions)	15 minutes
Groups share contribution answers to focus questions	30–40 minutes
Facilitator thanks participants for their time and attention	5 minutes
Total Time:	**1–1¼ hours**

# Creating Group Connections

Level of Difficulty:	Moderate to Challenging
Estimated Time:	2½–3 hours
Thinking Styles Utilized:	Analytics, Practicals, Relators, Possibilities

Synopsis:

In a large, complex change process, there are many groups in an organization that don't know each other very well. When the change process begins, they are often thrown together to work on a common project. The hope is that if you get smart, dedicated people together and tell them what the goals are, they will be able to work together as a cohesive team. Unfortunately, it doesn't work that way.

We have been in many organizations where different groups never get beyond their differences. They don't get to know each other and fail to utilize the diverse skills each possess, even if they are really smart.

In many organizations, there is a strong tendency to focus on the task part of a project and pay little attention to the process part (positive group climate, good communication, high levels of trust) of a change initiative. Unfortunately, it is in the process that things usually break down. Change facilitators need to have both discipline and courage if they are to change the natural focus and attention to the task only.

This design creates the opportunity to have a good "beginning" when two different groups get together. It engages all participants, values their contributions, and creates a database for understanding each other.

A facilitator works best with this design, ideally someone neutral who has some working knowledge of both groups and the institution. Do not have one person from one of the groups facilitate this meeting, because it will feel like "their" meeting instead of "our" meeting. An outside facilitator can keep everyone on task and it enables everyone to fully participate.

Facilitator Tip:

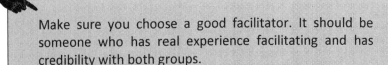

Make sure you choose a good facilitator. It should be someone who has real experience facilitating and has credibility with both groups.

Goals:

1. To create a shared database between two groups

2. To seek understanding about what matters/is important to two different groups

3. To begin to develop a constructive relationship between two different groups

Logistics:

Materials: Flip chart paper, easels, markers, paper, pens

Space Needs: Large, comfortable room with movable chairs

Number of Participants: 10 to 40 (for this activity, we will use 20 people, 10 in each group, as a model for this design)

The Activity:

1. Welcome participants and explain the purpose of the meeting. Everyone should briefly introduce themselves by name, role, and length of time with the company. It is important that participants get a feel for who is at the meeting.

2. Ask each group to get together and create five questions to ask the members of the other group. These questions should enable group members to get to know each other better and be thought-provoking, engaging, and penetrating. Give them 15 minutes for this task. Suggest that each group have a recorder for their questions.

   Suggest some questions before the groups begin their task to stimulate their thinking and give them some examples of the quality of the questions that are being sought.

   - What are three core values that your group/division truly "lives"?

   - What is it about your group that makes you feel proud about being a member?

   - What are some important things you have learned by working with other members of your group?

   - What are some regrets you might have about working with your group? What things could you be doing differently?

   - How would you describe the culture of your group?

   - Describe what communication looks like in your group.

   The idea is to craft questions that will enable participants to understand the complexities and nuances of the other group.

Facilitator Tip:

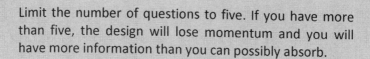

Limit the number of questions to five. If you have more than five, the design will lose momentum and you will have more information than you can possibly absorb.

3. After each group has generated their best five questions, have each group member choose a partner from the other group to interview (Group A members interview Group B members).

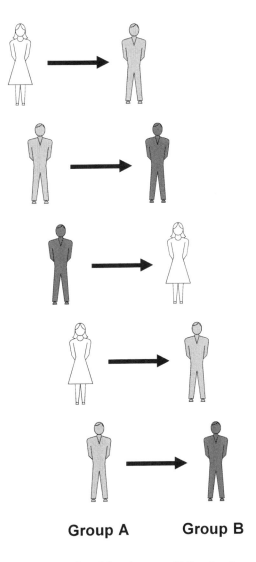

Group A   **Group B**

4. Ask the pairs to take 30 minutes (15 minutes per person) to interview their partner from the other group. Their goal is to have their partner answer the focus questions and for everyone to really listen carefully while interviewing. You want to get quality information from the interview and begin to establish some rapport between members.

5. After the interviews, give participants a brief break of 10 minutes.

6. After the interviews are completed, have the groups reconvene into their original group and give them 30 minutes to capture the major ideas and themes they heard from their partner interviews. Have them put this information on a flip chart because they are going to share what they learned about the other group in the next step.

The following might be a small example of a group's interview summary and learnings:

What are they proud of?
- They have an excellent reputation with customers
- They are on the cutting edge of their field
- Group members are hard working, smart, and honest in their dealings with one another
- They are willing to help anyone
- They have received a number of awards for excellence
- Projects are completed on time

How do they describe their culture?
- Open
- Friendly
- Conflict adverse
- People open to learning
- No big egos

How they describe communication in their group:
- Everyone is kept informed
- Overwhelming at times
- No secrets
- People take ownership for communicating with others
- People are honest in their communication

---

7. After each group has captured the essence of the personal interviews on flip charts, have each group present their information to the other group. Their goal is to share what they have learned about the other group. Each group should check for understanding and not rush through the presentations.

    This is not a data dump. Providing personal examples is helpful (e.g., "Your group talked about your team members' honesty with each other, even when sharing difficult information."). The goal is to convey both the substance of what was said in the interviews and the quality of the information.

8. After the presentations, check for understanding and clarification. Ask, "Do you feel that this information reflects your group appropriately? Is there anything that was missed or miscommunicated?" You want to make sure that group members feel understood and heard.

9. Once the presentations have been made, you have several options:

    a) Open up the floor to participants' general reactions to the shared information. (*What resonated? What discoveries were made?*)

    b) Facilitate a discussion about possibilities. (*Given what we have heard, what do we need to keep in mind as we continue to get to know each other? Work together?*)

    c) Have participants talk about the connections they see between the different groups/organizations. (*What are some possible roadblocks or challenges people see as they continue to work together?*)

    Keep the facilitated discussion to no more than 20 to 30 minutes. Remember, this is about creating a positive beginning. Do not rush for closure at this time. It would be helpful to schedule another meeting with this group as soon as possible to review purposes, create ground rules, and start working on the larger tasks.

SCHEDULE	
Facilitator welcomes participants and explains purpose of the meeting	10 minutes
Participants give brief (30 second) introductions of themselves	10–15 minutes
Groups create five questions for interviews	15 minutes
Group members pair off and conduct interviews	30 minutes
Break	10 minutes
Groups reconvene and distill information from the personal interviews	30 minutes
Each group presents what they have learned about the other group	20–30 minutes
Facilitator conducts open discussion about participants' reactions and possible next steps	20 minutes
Total Time:	**2½–3 hours**

# New Leader Assimilation

Level of Difficulty: Moderate

Estimated Time: 2½ hours

Thinking Styles Utilized: Practicals, Relators

Synopsis:

New leaders and their teams often face the same question: What do I really know about this leader or team? The new leader assimilation was developed by GE to provide leaders with a powerful way to hear firsthand what is of concern and interest. This process reflects a spirit of openness that can energize, focus, and create shared perspective. It should be used no sooner than 30 days after a new leader is assigned and is best done within 30 to 90 days.

Goals:

1. To promote integration and communication
2. To clarify expectations and requirements
3. To openly exchange views
4. To identify and provide recommendations
5. To clarify direction and objectives

Logistics:

Materials: Flip chart paper, easels, masking tape, Post-it® notes

Space Needs: Comfortable room with movable chairs and open wall space

Number of Participants: 6 to 15

The Activity:

This activity occurs in three phases:

- data gathering
- data integration and exchange
- capturing action items

1. With everyone together, review the objectives, agenda, and ground rules.

   Example:

Objectives	Agenda	Ground Rules
• Promote integration and communication • Clarify expectations and requirements • Openly exchange views • Identify and provide recommendations • Clarify direction and objectives	• Team meeting— 45 minutes • Leader review of data with facilitator— 30 minutes • Data integration and exchange— 30 minutes • Determine key actions— 15 minutes	• Anonymity • Confidentiality • Respect/honesty • Questions/ recommendations • Camaraderie and good faith

2. Have the team leader leave the room.

3. Ask the team questions like the ones listed below and record the answers on flip charts:

   - What do we appreciate about this leader?

   - What do we already know about this leader?

   - What don't we know but would like to know about this leader?

- What are our concerns about the team leader leading our team?

- What does the team leader most need to know about us as a group?

- What are the major problems the team leader will be facing during the first three to six months?

- What are the major challenges this team will be facing over the next year?

- What are some specific suggestions we have for overcoming the challenges mentioned above?

Example:

What do we appreciate?	**What we don't know but would like to...**	**What he needs to know about us as a group...**
• High energy • Talking about his/her family • Ownership • Doing this exercise	• Why he left ABC company • What his/her top three criteria for excellence are • The last person he fired and why	• We really care about our work • This is our 4th leader in 3 years • We want to be successful

4. The team leader is in another room answering many of the same questions but from the perspective of "what the team leader knows/wants to know about this team." For example:

- What is your leadership style?

- What traits do you admire in leaders you know or have known?

- What do you expect from individuals as a team member?

- What do you appreciate about the team members? Provide some examples.

- What have you learned about this team's strengths? Its weaknesses?

175

- How do you describe the culture of this group/organization? What makes you describe it in those terms?

- What do I need to know most about how this group/team operates?

- What are some of the major problems you see this team facing over the next several months?

- What challenges do you see coming?

5. Bring the leader back to the room. Have the leader review the charts and prepare to respond to, comment on, or ask questions about the information generated by the team. Set up the session so that this 30-minute segment is when the team is eating lunch.

6. Bring the team back to the room where you and the team leader are prepared to begin the session to exchange and integrate the information. After a "welcome back," review the ground rules once again. This is important to ensure a positive, productive climate and underscores the importance of transparency and trust.

Ground rules for the session:

- **Anonymity.** When the information is presented, it is a team output. No one person should be addressed, focused on, or questioned about the items.

- **Confidentiality.** This speaks to not only keeping things within the team, but also how this information will be used. Confidentiality is an important contribution to a climate of honesty and openness—without it, the session will become a "show."

- **Respect and honesty.** In this exercise, everyone has an equal voice. That means everyone's voice is heard and no one dominates.

- **Questions/recommendations.** Sometimes, when addressing some of the questions, team members might have a tendency to blame or point fingers. Remind participants this is meant to focus on questions and recommendations—not cause or blame.

- **Camaraderie and good faith.** The power of intention to build relationships and to do the right thing are key drivers in this exercise. If it gets too intense, refocus the team on camaraderie and good faith.

7. Prepare the team leader and the team to review the information and address questions. Typically, team members will share responsibility for presenting sections of the information. Where possible, the team leader probes for understanding and answers questions. Then switch the focus and have the team leader address any remaining questions and discuss his/her responses (not already addressed in the team round).

8. Lead an open discussion that is focused on the top three to five recommendations and/or action items based on what has been discussed and discovered.

Example:

Action Items

- We will have three team meetings/offsites per year focusing on team development.

- We will work together to develop 5 to 6 success outcomes for our department.

- We will institute every-other-week staff meetings.

SCHEDULE	
Facilitator welcomes participants and explains purpose of the meeting	5 minutes
Facilitator asks questions of the team without the team leader present and records responses on a flip chart; the team leader is in another room answering the same or similar questions	45 minutes
Facilitator and team leader meet to review the information; team goes to lunch	30 minutes
Team and team leader come back together and facilitator holds integration and information exchange session	45 minutes
Facilitator helps group capture and work any action items resulting from agreement	20 minutes
Total Time:	**2½ hours**

# Team Effectiveness Check-In Discussion*

Level of Difficulty:	Easy
Estimated Time:	1 hour
Thinking Styles Utilized:	Analytics, Practicals, Relators

Synopsis:

Teams are more and more a part of everyday life. Since what happens on a team occurs within a dynamic context, things can and do change. Building in the discipline of a structured team check-in discussion allows team members to understand the impact of the team's behavior on the performance of the team and to discuss what behaviors need to be managed. This tool should be used on a regular basis to allow teams to proactively manage team norms rather than waiting until the team is in trouble. For the team effectiveness check-in to be most effective, the team will already have developed norms or guidelines. While a high degree of trust is optimal, this exercise can be done with teams on their way to building a high degree of trust.

Goals:

1. To allow team members to have a structured dialogue around specific performance elements that are meeting or not meeting their expectations

2. To enhance awareness and trust among team members

3. To create clarity and understanding of similar and different points of view

*Adapted from Marshall Goldsmith, *Team Building Without Time Waiting.*

179

Logistics:

Materials: Flip chart paper, easels, markers

Space Needs: Meeting room of any size

Number of Participants: 6 to 12

The Activity:

This activity can be done without a facilitator and can be led by either a team leader or team member. The questions below can be used to facilitate the discussion session. Responses should be recorded on a flip chart.

1. Start the team check-in discussion session by stating "Thinking about the cohesiveness and productivity of our team, note your ratings on the following with (1 = not meeting expectations at all and 10 = far exceeding expectations)." Please note that the aspects being rated can be selected by the leader and the team and could include operating principles, values, or other agreed-to guidelines.

2. The facilitator records the scores on the chart, which is visible to the whole team. There should be little or no discussion at this point, only the recording of the numbers. In addition, ask the group to use only whole numbers—no 5.75s! Your flip chart should look like this:

Team Functioning	Your Ratings
Communication and Information Exchange	6, 7, 6, 2, 10
Team Member Participation	7, 5, 3, 6, 8
Meeting Effectiveness	8, 8, 8, 6, 9
Team Leadership	8, 8, 8, 8, 8
Roles and Responsibilities of Team Members	6, 5, 6, 7, 6

3. Have one member of the group tally the scores to come up with average scores. Below is an example of what your flip chart should look like:

Team Functioning	Your Ratings	Average
Communication and Information Exchange	6, 7, 6, 2, 10	6.2
Team Member Participation	7, 5, 3, 6, 8	5.8
Meeting Effectiveness	8, 8, 8, 6, 9	7.8
Team Leadership	8, 8, 8, 8, 8	8.0
Roles and Responsibilities of Team Members	6, 5, 6, 7, 6	6.0

4. Have the team leader/member facilitate a discussion with some or all of the following questions:

   - What seems to be working well? Why?

   - What areas do we agree on?

   - What are the areas of biggest difference in scores among our team?

   - How can we address the differences in scores from current state to "needs to be" state?

   - How can we address those differences? What are one to two actions we can agree on to move ahead?

5. Have the facilitator record the information from the discussion focusing on the question, "What are the one to two actions we can agree on to move ahead?" For example:

   - We need to ensure that *everyone* participates in group meetings and decision making.

- Let's make sure we clarify everyone's roles and expectations before we start working.

- Make sure we include everyone on group minutes and team phone calls.

- Our leadership is doing really well—let's not forget this!

SCHEDULE

Team leader or member calls team together for check-in meeting and explains purpose	5 minutes
Team leader/member asks team members to respond to questions and records on flip chart	15 minutes
Team leader/member holds discussion about scores, differences among the team, and differences in current state vs. needs to be	20–35 minutes
Team leader/member solicits one to two action items	10 minutes
Total Time:	**Approximately 1 hour**

Facilitator Tip:

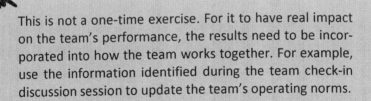

This is not a one-time exercise. For it to have real impact on the team's performance, the results need to be incorporated into how the team works together. For example, use the information identified during the team check-in discussion session to update the team's operating norms.

Chapter 6
Toolbox

This section provides several collaborative tools and techniques that can be used on their own or to support the designs in this book. All of them are rather easy to use and encourage collaboration and participation. They enable meeting leaders and participants to move toward transparent outcomes.

Some of the tools enhance collaboration, others help a group make a final decision, and still others support effective group management.

The tools and techniques included in this section are:

- Brainstorming
- Las Vegas Voting
- Mind Mapping
- Constructive Feedback
- Nominal Group Technique
- Parking Lot
- Self-Managed Groups
- Meeting Evaluation Guide

Brainstorming

Synopsis:

Brainstorming is one of the most widely used and often abused tools for developing information. It was originated in 1938 by Alex Osburn. Brainstorming is a group technique for generating information that involves the spontaneous contribution of ideas from all group members. The primary focus of this technique is to get ideas out on the table rather than to critically analyze the ideas. Synergy often occurs because the list of ideas generated by the group is usually much longer and more creative than the sum total of ideas that would have been contributed by each of the individual group members. Brainstorming engages participants' thinking in new and exciting ways. It generates alternative approaches to solving problems or accomplishing goals using creativity and thinking beyond our self-imposed frameworks.

Goals:

1. To create opportunity for all participants to share their ideas

2. To give participants the opportunity to engage in a creative problem-solving exercise

Logistics:

Materials: Flip chart paper, easels, markers, masking tape

Space Needs: Comfortable room where participants can move about freely

Number of Participants: 5 to 10, but can easily be used for groups of up to 20 participants

The Activity:

1. Define the brainstorming topic before the session. It should be clearly focused (e.g., How can we increase our global marketplace presence?).

2. Begin the session by providing brief background information about the topic and why it is important for this group's attention.

3. Write the topic on a flip chart so that it can be clearly seen by all participants.

4. Present the guidelines for brainstorming and have them posted in full view:

Evaluation and judgment are forbidden (no criticism allowed)

The quantity of ideas is important (don't edit your ideas)

Wild, far-fetched, and illogical ideas are encouraged

Ideas may be combined, modified, or piggybacked (this is highly encouraged)

5. Before the brainstorming begins, ask participants to turn to the person next to them and share some of their ideas for a minute or so. This will help stimulate ideas and encourage participation.

6. Ask participants to call out their ideas.

7. Write all ideas on the flip chart. Do not discuss them.

Facilitator Tips:

1) When the ideas are recorded, the writing should be large enough that every participant can easily see what ideas have been generated.

2) Once an idea has been recorded, especially if it represents a complex thought, it is a good practice to confirm whether the recorded idea reflects the idea that was intended.

3) While the ideas are recorded, they should not be edited by anyone. All ideas should be listed using, as closely as possible, the actual words of the individual who contributed the idea.

4) To be effective, any brainstorming process must enable the participants to generate their ideas without fear of criticism. This will create a climate where all ideas are acceptable and that no one will be looked upon unfavorably for voicing an idea, thought, or opinion that may not have popular support.

5) Research shows that the last 25% of the ideas generated in a brainstorming session are of higher quality than the first 75%! When we begin to generate ideas, we usually come up with the usual or easy ideas first. Hang in there and push people on to continually generate ideas.

6) We have found that it is useful to use different colored markers to write the ideas. Colors stimulate thinking and creativity.

8. End brainstorming when you have sufficient ideas. Fifteen minutes should be the maximum time.

9. After the group has generated a list of ideas, you, as the facilitator, have several options:

   a) Look for the meaningful combination of ideas.

   b) Eliminate ideas that are not relevant to the topic or not realistic (cost too much; organization doesn't have the capacity; something that was tried before and failed miserably; etc.).

   c) Use Las Vegas Voting (see page 191) to prioritize the most interesting or promising ideas.

10. It is important to provide closure to the session. Prioritizing the list can help do this, but it is important to let participants know how the information will be used. If possible, follow up with the participants to inform them how their ideas were utilized.

SAMPLE SCHEDULE	
Facilitator provides brief background information about the topic and writes the topic on a flip chart so that it can be seen by all participants	3–5 minutes
Facilitator presents guidelines for brainstorming and has them in full view	2–3 minutes
Participants turn to the person next to them and share some of their ideas	2 minutes
Participants call out their ideas and facilitator writes all ideas on a flip chart—the group does not discuss them	10 minutes
Facilitator uses one of the options in Step 9 and closes out the session	5 minutes
Total Time:	**Approximately 25 minutes**

Alternatives:

Use a structured brainstorming approach that has the same basic rules as brainstorming, except for the following:

1. Use a round-robin format so that each person has a chance to contribute.

2. Allow any participant to "pass" on any round.

The benefit of this approach is that it brings out the quieter participants and presents domination by the loudest or more powerful participants. One drawback is that it can create pressure to contribute.

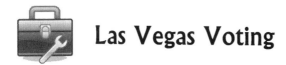

Las Vegas Voting

Synopsis:

Participative and engaging meetings produce many ideas and suggestions. This, in turn, creates lengthy lists for the group to manage and prioritize. This technique—sometimes referred to as multivoting—provides a starting point by quickly showing everyone which ideas have top priority. It has the added benefits of being open, democratic, fair, and transparent.

Logistics:

Materials: Flip chart paper, easels, markers, sticky dots (found at any stationery or office supply store)

Number of Participants: Almost any size group (10 to 100)

The Activity:

1. After the group has developed a list of activities or issues to be prioritized, explain that each participant has five votes to distribute among the ideas on the list. Participants should vote for the ideas they believe will be the best ones to consider and implement. They can weigh their votes in any way; for example, they can place all five votes on one idea, place two votes on one idea, and three on another, or vote once for five different ideas.

2. Give each participant five sticky dots to place on the flip chart next to the idea(s) they prefer. If you don't have sticky dots, participants can vote with their fingers: To give a particular idea two votes, they would hold up two fingers. Count the votes as each idea is read aloud and mark the total in view of everyone. Typically, in a few minutes, everyone will have a sense of the top three or four ideas.

3. If many items on a list receive an even number of votes, conduct a second round of voting with three votes per person. This second vote will clarify the priorities because participants can't spread their votes around as much.

Facilitator Tip:

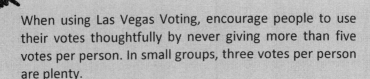

When using Las Vegas Voting, encourage people to use their votes thoughtfully by never giving more than five votes per person. In small groups, three votes per person are plenty.

How to Enhance Communication across the Company

1. Develop web portal ✓✓✓✓✓✓✓

2. Survey on specific issues on a weekly basis ✓✓

3. Develop multilevel communications committee ✓✓

4. Create intramural softball team ✓✓✓

5. Start "Breakfast with the CEO" ✓✓✓✓ ✓✓✓✓✓✓

6. Develop a coffee bar in the cafeteria ✓✓✓✓

Mind Mapping

Synopsis:

Mind Mapping, created and popularized by Tony Buzan in *Use Both Sides of Your Brain* (1991), is the visual depiction of an idea, concept, or issue. It taps both the left and right sides of the brain, helping organize information and thought processes without stifling new and different ideas. Use it to

- Stimulate the creative thinking of stakeholders in a meeting;
- Diagnose the complexity of a problem or issue; and
- Capture a lot of ideas and then organize them coherently.

Enabling participants to "map" out the complexity of a problem or issue will generate far more ideas than traditional linear listing. It also gives people the opportunity to build on the contributions of others and see connections between ideas they wouldn't see on a long list of brainstormed ideas.

You can use mind mapping for project planning, defining goals, action planning, note taking, identifying values, or creative problem solving. Everyone's ideas are captured on the mind map because all ideas are considered valid and are not judged.

A traditional mind map usually limits the ideas created to one word. The adaptation outlined below captures the essence of what people suggest, not just one word, which makes it more productive.

Goals:

1. To fully engage participants' thinking
2. To map out the complexity of a problem or issue
3. To show the interconnectedness of ideas created

Logistics:

Materials: Flip chart paper, easels, markers, masking tape

Space Needs: A room large enough for participants to move about freely

Number of Participants: Up to 50 (if you have more than 50, have two facilitators and two mind maps)

The Activity:

1. Tape several sheets of flip chart paper to a wall—the larger the papered area, the better—to form the mind map.

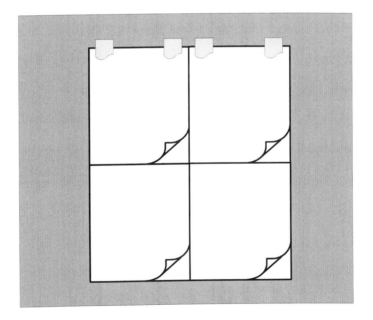

2. In the center of the mind map, state a central theme or problem (e.g., How can we further improve company morale?). Tell participants that the goal is to generate as many ideas as possible to address the focus question or central issue.

3. Ask participants to "pair and share"—pair up with the next person and talk about the issue or question to generate ideas and energy.

4. After two minutes, have participants call out their ideas in a brainstorming fashion. Remember that all ideas are valid, so write down what people say. Print the words on a line and make sure the lines are connected to the major theme in the center. As the ideas are generated, ask participants if the ideas stand by themselves or are part of another idea.

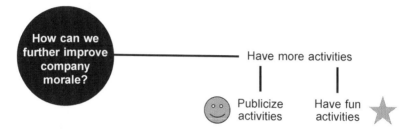

5. Use different colors of markers when drawing the mind map. Colors stimulate thinking and creativity. You can also use pictures and images to capture an idea. The images don't have to be artistic or beautiful as long as people understand what they represent.

6. Continue capturing all the ideas until everyone is finished, and then ask participants to observe a minute of silence. After a minute has passed, ask the group if anyone has more ideas. (The minute of silence usually produces several more ideas and might even jumpstart a new series of ideas and connections.)

Your final mind map might look like the one on the following page.

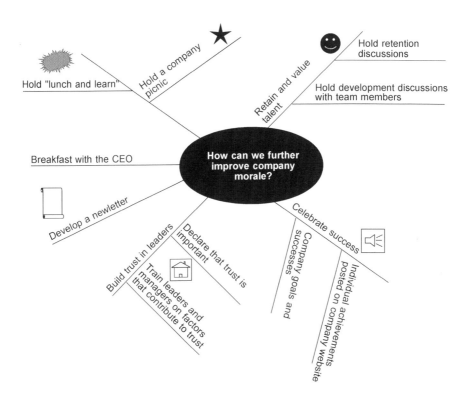

Mind map: How can we further improve company morale?

- Hold "lunch and learn"
- Hold a company picnic
- Retain and value talent
  - Hold retention discussions
  - Hold development discussions with team members
- Breakfast with the CEO
- Develop a newletter
- Build trust in leaders
  - Declare that trust is important
  - Train leaders and managers on factors that contribute to trust
- Celebrate success
  - Company goals and successes
  - Individual achievements posted on company website

SAMPLE SCHEDULE	
Facilitator introduces concept and idea or question	2–5 minutes
Participants pair and share	2 minutes
Facilitator creates mind map	15–20 minutes
Participants observe moment of silence	1–2 minutes
Facilitator asks for additional comments/ideas	5 minutes
Total Time:	**30–35 minutes**

Facilitator Tip:

> After completing the mind map, you may want to use Las Vegas Voting (in the Toolbox section) to prioritize the ideas. That will enable you to reduce a sizeable number of ideas (30 to 50) to a manageable number (between 5 and 10).

Alternatives:

Mind mapping has become easy to do using technology. Programs, some of which are free, make capturing, changing, and documenting mind maps easy. Freemind is downloadable at no cost, and Mindjet developed Mindmanager, and it is available at a minimal cost.

Constructive Feedback

Synopsis:

During a collaborative change process, there will be many opportunities to present ideas and solicit feedback. Many of the meeting designs in this book actively solicit feedback from stakeholders. Feedback creates the opportunity to enhance ideas and provides a reality check on the practicality of suggestions and ideas.

Unfortunately, there is a downside to feedback that needs to be managed by the collaborative leader. We have witnessed planning groups, task forces, and steering committees making presentations to others within the organization and see the feedback process become a critical and demoralizing process. What should have been an opportunity to build and strengthen ideas becomes a "turkey shoot" where the criticals prevail and ideas, even people, are personally destroyed. Once you have experienced a meeting like this, enthusiasm for future presentations quickly fades.

Negative feedback rarely improves the quality of ideas but continues to persist. The challenge for the collaborative leader is to create a constructive feedback process where criticism has its place but does not become the overriding factor in a discussion of ideas. The goal is to obtain effective and honest feedback and create both emotional and intellectual safety in the process.

The beauty of this technique is that it gets everyone's ideas in the room, especially the less verbal participants. It also neutralizes the power of the critics while getting their ideas in the room.

Goals:

1. To provide constructive feedback to proposed ideas/recommendations

2. To fully involve participants in improving ideas

Logistics:

Materials: Flip chart paper, easels, markers, masking tape, 5" × 7", Post-it® notes

Space Needs: Comfortable room where participants can move about freely

Number of Participants: 10 to 50 participants (in this example, there will be 15 participants who have been working in small groups on an issue and are ready to present their ideas to others in the larger group)

The Activity:

1. When participants are ready to make their presentations, the facilitator informs everyone before the presentations are made that the feedback process is going to be a little different.

2. Make sure that all participants have some large (5" × 7") Post-its®, about 10 to 12 per participant. Inform everyone that they should use the Post-its® to write down their feedback regarding the presentations. Their written feedback can address any of the following three elements:

   a) What participants like about the ideas presented by others. It is always nice to hear what people appreciate about ideas, so encourage this (e.g., "Your idea of having a weekly breakfast meeting between the Plant Manager and floor operators is just what we need.").

   b) Resources to share. This could include people's names, suggested contacts, books, research that would help leverage or enhance the effectiveness of the suggested ideas or plans presented (e.g., "You should contact Jim Seitz in Marketing, he is an expert on this topic." "There is a web portal, Thinknext, which is an excellent source of ideas on this topic.").

   c) Suggestions to improve the ideas presented (e.g., "You suggest that different groups meet with the Senior Leadership Team on a regular basis. I believe they should visit different site locations rather than have everyone come to them" or "Your communication plan seems very one way. You need to build in more interaction where plant personnel have the opportunity to provide feedback and ideas.").

It is always helpful to provide examples so that the participants clearly understand what kind of feedback you seek.

Facilitator Tip:

In a group with low trust or one that is very new at collaborative practices, this is an excellent way to solicit feedback in a nonthreatening way. As stakeholders get used to being more open, you can try a more direct approach where you solicit verbal feedback from participants.

3. Let participants know that after each presentation, several minutes will be provided so that they can write down their feedback on Post-its®. After they have written their feedback, have them place the Post-its® on the appropriate flip chart page. Then have the next presentation (this should take no more than two to four minutes per presentation).

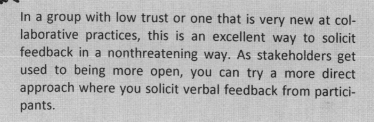

4. Continue the process of presentation, time for written feedback, and placing Post-its® until all the presentations are completed and feedback provided.

5. The final step is to have each presenting group meet for 15 to 20 minutes to read the feedback on the Post-its®, react to the feedback, and reach beginning agreement on how to include the suggestions for improvement and resource ideas, where appropriate.

6. If possible, have each group make a brief (two minutes) presentation to the larger group to show how the feedback and suggestions helped/influenced their thinking.

Facilitator Tip:

It is helpful to use the same three elements in the same sequence: (1) things you like about the idea, (2) resources to share, and (3) suggestions for improvement. The structured sequence ensures that individuals do not go to what is wrong with the ideas right away!

Nominal Group Technique

Synopsis:

The Nominal Group Technique (NGT) is one of the classic decision-making tools that has been around for a long time. What makes this tool so effective is that it neutralizes the impact of dominant participants and different levels of power in a meeting (e.g., having vice presidents and middle level managers in a strategy meeting).

The NGT ensures anonymity regarding the generation and scoring of ideas. No one knows who is suggesting an idea, so the ideas are evaluated on their own merit and not prone to organizational dynamics (e.g., someone's role, position, length of experience, status in the group, or "personality").

We will describe an adaptation of a traditional NGT approach and share an alternative that can be used in meetings where the participants work well together.

Goals:

1. To neutralize the impact of personalities and power in a decision-making process

2. To create a transparent structure to evaluate ideas and recommendations based on their merit

Logistics:

Materials: Flip chart paper, easels, markers, index cards, pens, pencils

Space Needs: Comfortable room with plenty of usable wall space

Number of Participants: 5 to 10

The Activity:

1. Communicate the primary purpose of the meeting to all participants (e.g., "Today we are here to identify ways the Marketing and Sales departments can work together more collaboratively.").

2. Provide 5 to 10 index cards for each participant and suggest that they capture their ideas on the index card (limit one suggestion per card). This should take 7 to 10 minutes. (No names are used on the cards.)

3. Collect all the cards, shuffle them up, and then record them in full view of the group. (It might be helpful to ask some meeting participants for help in recording the suggestions to move along this part of the meeting.) Note redundancies by checking them off as you create the list. Your initial list might look like this:

1. Have them go on a team-building retreat together.
2. Build in a performance goal that rewards collaboration between two groups.
3. Interview key members of both groups and determine what the problems are.
4. Have the president meet with the VP of Sales and the VP of Marketing to discuss this issue and resolve it.
5. Have key members from each group discuss ways to work together more effectively ASAP.
6. Somehow show how working together is going to help us make more money.

4. After all the ideas are captured on a flip chart in full view, clarify the suggestions to ensure everyone *understands* them. This is not the time to evaluate the ideas, just understand them. There is no judgment or feedback involved in this step. (Keep this as brief as possible.)

5. After the creation and clarification steps, it is time to determine the best ideas. Ask each participant to vote for or rank what they believe are the best five ideas (this is different than a traditional NGT that would rank all the ideas on the list). By limiting their "votes," each participant has to select carefully, which is what you want them to do.

6. Communicate the following scoring system: "Everyone has only five votes. Please give your best choice the number 5, give a 4 to your next best idea, all the way to 1 for your least favorite, best idea."

7. Have the participants do their voting silently and anonymously on a piece of paper. Once again, collect the sheets, shuffle them, and record the "votes" in full view of everyone. For example, for eight participants in this exercise, the final list might look like this:

Idea #

1	= 3-3-2-2-1	(11)
2	= 5-3-3-5-2-1-5-4-5-5	(38)
3	= 2-2-3	(7)
4	= 1-2	(3)
5	= 2-2-1-4	(9)
6	= 1-3	(4)

Facilitator Tip:

> Give the meeting participants a short break (5–7 minutes) as they tally the votes.

8. Total the scores and this will determine what the best ideas are. As you can see, suggestion #2 received 38 votes; #1 received 11 votes; and #5 received 9 votes.

9. At this time, there are several options: (1) thank people for their participation and close the meeting because you accomplished your primary purpose of identifying the best ideas; (2) have an open discussion about possible next steps regarding the top priority recommendations (keep this to 15 minutes); or (3) have an open discussion regarding participants' reaction to the proposed ideas (e.g., "Are these practical?" "Where should we go with these?" "What do you think about the priority ideas?" "Are we missing anything?").

SAMPLE SCHEDULE	
Facilitator welcomes participants and communicates the purpose of the meeting	10 minutes
Participants create suggestions and put them on index cards	10 minutes
Facilitator collects the index cards and records suggestions in full view on flip chart paper	10–15 minutes
Facilitator clarifies the suggestions	5–10 minutes
Participants "vote" for their five choices	10 minutes
Facilitator records votes in full view of participants	10 minutes
Total Time:	**Approximately 1 hour**

If you have a brief discussion about the priority ideas, you would limit this to 15 to 20 minutes.

Facilitator Tip:

> If you decide to have a brief discussion about the priority ideas, this is a judgment call on your part. If you are working with a "difficult" group, be careful about your choice.

With the Alternative noted below, you save about 10 minutes, where participants verbally present their ideas and vote.

Alternative:

If the trust level in a particular group is high or the group has a good experience working together, you can adapt this meeting in several ways:

1. After explaining the purpose of the discussion, have participants take 10 minutes to write down their ideas.

2. Then, using a round-robin approach, verbally take one idea from each participant and record in full view. After the list is created, clarify any of the suggestions that need to be clarified.

3. Have the participants capture their five "votes" on paper and then verbally share their rankings with each other. (It is important **not** to discuss *how* someone ranked a particular item.) Capture the rankings in full view. At this time, you have a prioritized list.

Parking Lot

Synopsis:

In high-energy meetings, smart, energized participants often wander away from the original purpose or the agreed-upon agenda. Suddenly, participants may find themselves discussing an idea or issue that has nothing to do with the agenda. They may mumble, "What's going on here?" "Why are we talking about strategic planning in a meeting to improve company morale?"

Once a group wanders off, you may find it difficult to get everyone back on track. This is especially true when the group includes strong egos, a revered participant, or a respected leader. What can a participant possibly say when the leader takes the discussion in a different direction from the meeting's purpose?

This time-tested technique, sometimes called the "Grass Catcher" or "Bike Rack," captures the important yet off-topic ideas rather than letting them take the group off on a tangent. Quite simply, this technique "parks" tangential ideas on a sheet of flip chart paper so that participants can return to them after completing the task at hand. It's particularly useful for groups that meet regularly, such as customer service groups, technology groups, or leadership teams.

Logistics:

Materials: Flip chart paper, easels, magic markers

Space Needs: Comfortable room where participants can move about freely

Number of Participants: 5 to 20

The Activity:

1. Confirm the general purpose of the meeting before it begins. Say, for example, "Today, we are working on improving company morale" or "The primary purpose of this meeting is to prepare for the strategic planning meeting we're having next week."

2. Let all participants know that you will be using a Parking Lot tool to capture important ideas that may arise during the meeting but have little to do with its stated purpose. For example: "Our purpose is to find ways to improve morale. We don't want to ignore a particular problem that may come up about a plant, but that problem doesn't fit with the purpose of the meeting. So we will capture the plant problem on a flip chart and, before we leave, agree upon a next step for it."

3. Emphasize that the Parking Lot issues will be addressed and not forgotten. Be sure to leave at least 15 minutes toward the end of the meeting to address any issues in the Parking Lot. Say, for example, two unrelated issues came up during a meeting about plant morale.

4. As recorded by the facilitator, the Parking Lot might look like this:

Parking Lot

Issue: The physical plant people have reported continuous equipment breakdowns.
Action: John will talk with the plant director and come up with a list of issues and proposed solutions by the end of the month.

Issue: The newsletter isn't being distributed to all the divisions.
Action: Mary will contact our communication director this afternoon to validate this claim and solve the problem by the end of the week.

Self-Managed Groups

Synopsis:

Many times a large group of participants (20 to 60) can be divided into smaller, more manageable groups of five to seven participants. The facilitator may give them a specific task such as, "Please take the next 20 minutes to brainstorm ways to improve communication throughout the home office" or "In the next 45 minutes, please discuss the four recommendations from our self-study on diversity. Be prepared to report back ways to implement the four recommendations." Visiting all the groups to ensure they are using their time well and to resolve any disputes will quickly exhaust the facilitator.

Self-managed groups will leverage the time and productivity of large groups. Use them in the following situations:

- Several groups are working simultaneously on a task or a large number of participants in a meeting divide into smaller groups for a meaningful discussion.

- You want to provide a structure for groups to accomplish a certain task and be fully responsible for the outcome of their work.

Goals:

1. To have participants take responsibility for their work
2. To create the appropriate structure for groups to accomplish their task

Logistics:

Materials: Handout explaining the roles

Space Needs: Comfortable room where participants can move about freely

Number of Participants: 10 to 50

The Activity:

1. Tell participants that each group they form will be self-managing—in other words, responsible for its own work product and process. Note that you won't be checking on them, although you will be available to clarify the task.

2. Let all participants know that they need to identify people within their small work groups to take responsibility for one role. This should be done *before* the group starts work.

3. Distribute a handout summarizing the various roles. When assigning a task to a large group to work on in smaller, mixed groups, give them the self-managed roles handout at the end of this section before they go into their small groups to work.

4. Note the roles required by the particular task. You may want to review the various roles and their respective responsibilities using the following notes for guidance:

    -   The **recorder** captures the group's work on the flip chart. The facilitator may want to suggest that people assigned to record the group's work don't become trapped in traditional roles. If, for example, the work group includes an administrative assistant she/he should not automatically be assigned the role of recorder.

    -   The **presenter** shares the small group's work with all participants. Many people will want this high-profile role, but top leaders should avoid it. Suggest that other people volunteer to serve as the group's presenter.

    -   The **timekeeper** gently reminds the group of how much time it has to accomplish the task. About every 10 or 15 minutes, the timekeeper should alert the group to how much time remains. (This is a great role for top leaders, provided they only remind people and don't aggravate them.)

    -   The **facilitator** makes sure that all the participants are engaged and involved and that everything remains on track so that the group can accomplish the end task. This can involve managing a dominant personality who may start taking over the group. Because verbal people often volunteer for this role, you might want to deliver this message: "The role of facilitator is challenging. The main purpose is to ensure that everyone in the group participates. If you are doing a lot of talking, you are not facilitating!"

5. As participants move into their smaller work groups, remind them to assign the roles right after the entire group has congregated and *before* any work begins.

Self-Managed Roles
Description Handout

Recorder: Captures the group's work on a flip chart

Presenter: Shares the group's work with all participants

Timekeeper: Gently reminds the group of how much time it has to accomplish the task

Facilitator: Makes sure all participants are engaged and involved; ensures everything remains on track so that the group can accomplish the end task

The Meeting Evaluation Guide

Synopsis:

One of the best ways to improve meeting effectiveness is to periodically and anonymously assess how participants experience the meeting. The following evaluation form should be distributed to meeting participants directly after they have conducted a meeting. In this way, their impressions and opinions are fresh and relevant.

Simply hand out this evaluation form and ask participants to take two to three minutes (that's all it takes) to complete it. Make sure that you ensure anonymity so that you get people's honest responses.

Collect the evaluation forms and organize the data as soon as you can. Make sure that everyone gets a summary report so that they understand how others experienced the meeting. The answers to these five simple questions will give you all the information you need to improve the quality of future meetings.

Conducting this kind of assessment on a periodic basis communicates several things to meeting participants:

- that their opinion is valued

- that the meeting leader is open to feedback

- that learning is part of the meeting journey and that quality information will further improve the group's meeting effectiveness

- that meetings are valuable to the organization and worthy of ongoing assessment to determine the value add of each meeting

These are all important messages to convey.

This simple evaluation form, when used appropriately, can be one of the most effective tools for leaders that we know about.

Meeting Evaluation Form

1. How *effective* was the meeting (did it accomplish your purpose?) Use a 1 to 10 scale. It is important to show average and range.

    1   2   3   4   5   6   7   8   9   10

    Not Effective   Very Effective

2. How involved did you feel? Show average and range.

    1   2   3   4   5   6   7   8   9   10

    Not Involved   Very Involved

3. What did you like most about the meeting?

    _____

    _____

    _____

    _____

    _____

4. What advice do you have to improve future meetings?

    _____

    _____

    _____

    _____

    _____

5. Feedback, comments, suggestions:

    _____

    _____

    _____

    _____

218

 # Appendix

How the Appendix Is Organized

Section 1: Why Meetings Don't Work

Over the past 25 years, we have identified the top ten reasons why most meetings are not effective. Any leader, facilitator, or consultant who wants to design and deliver effective meetings needs to deeply understand the key hurdles to productive meetings.

This list can be helpful for groups and teams that spend much of their time in meetings. It doesn't take much time to read and is easy to understand. It usually creates a great discussion among meeting participants. Many are motivated to avoid these traps after reading these ideas and will work mightily toward better meetings.

Section 2: Some Thoughts about Facilitation

This section provides excellent advice about the art and craft of meeting facilitation. Once again, the ideas are easy to understand, practice, and implement. Facilitation can be challenging, but the information gleaned in this section will be invaluable for both beginners and veterans.

Section 3: The Highly Effective Meeting Profile©*

This excellent assessment will enable you to diagnose any ongoing meeting that you lead, facilitate, or participate in. It is easy to utilize and will provide deep insight into how the assessed meeting actually works.

---

* Sanaghan, Goldstein, & Conway. Amherst, MA: HRD Press. (2003).

It looks at the five key elements at every meeting:

1. Decision making
2. Results orientation
3. Group climate
4. Procedures and protocols
5. Participation and engagement

Participants take the 50-question survey anonymously and produce a powerful visual that shows the strengths and weaknesses of the identified meeting.

Section 4: 27 Ways to Improve Your Meetings

This section provides wise and practical ideas and strategies to improve the quality and outcome of meetings. Gleaned from facilitating thousands of meetings, the information will prove to be invaluable to those individuals who are dedicated to learning how to have great meetings.

Why Meetings Don't Work

The Top Reasons Meetings Fail

1. The same people dominate the meeting.

Most of the time we can predict who the "talkers" will be in any meeting. These "talkers" tend to speak rather than to listen; share their opinions openly and often; fight resistance to their ideas and will bully others who get in their way. In short, they are a pain the rear.

The challenge for a meeting leader or facilitator is to neutralize the impact of the "talkers" and hear all the voices of the participants. The designs in this book show you how to neutralize the "dominators."

2. The critics win the day.

This is one of our favorites! We have witnessed hundreds of meetings where a strong critic stifles participation, creativity, and engagement. In our culture, people often get credit for being critical in a meeting! It is a sad thing to see a powerful critic ruin a meeting in the name of "bottom-line thinking" or "reality-based thinking."

3. They are predictable and boring.

When was the last time you were in an interesting and creative meeting where you felt all the participants were productive and well-utilized? Most people attend meetings with little enthusiasm or interest. Within the first ten minutes, everyone knows where the meeting is going and what probably won't be accomplished. We put little time in planning up front for an engaging meeting. We assume that somehow everyone will participate, share ideas, and achieve constructive results. Boring meetings rarely accomplish this.

4. There are unclear purposes and objectives for the meeting.

Too many meetings wander off as they generate too many ideas that never get thought through, let alone implemented. It is essential to have a clear focus and purpose for a meeting, even a creative problem-solving meeting.

5. Most managers and leaders have not been trained in group dynamics, meeting management, or facilitation.

Our institutions of higher education rarely have courses in these critical areas. Executives are expected somehow to "know" how to run a meeting. Meetings are complex animals. People come to the table with all kinds of aspirations, mental models, biases, need for power and control, different learning styles, avoidance of conflict—the list could go on and on.

Why do we pretend that the complexities people bring to the table shouldn't be considered when planning and facilitating a meeting?

6. Real participation and involvement are not encouraged.

The assumption that underlies most meetings is that all you have to do is put the right people in the room and have a clear purpose, and everyone will participate. This is rarely true. We often hear from managers and leaders, "If people have something to say, they will say it." Wrong. This only applies to the "overly verbal" participants who love to share their thoughts and ideas. What do you do with shy people? How do you manage different levels of power in the room? How do you manage various learning styles? Real participation takes planning.

7. Time bounded and linear thinkers tend to run most meetings.

Time is a precious resource. Everyone wants to utilize their time effectively. Too often, there is an unnecessary sense of urgency in most meetings. People are afraid to stop the train even if it is moving in the wrong direction!

There is way too much focus on keeping to the agenda, no matter what, allotting unrealistic time frames to discussing issues and getting to the end of the meeting as soon as possible. Meetings don't have to be tense affairs, rushing headlong to an artificial deadline.

8. The balance of task and relationship is not where it should be.

Many meetings are mainly task focused. Yet often, derailers occur as a result of poor dynamics, personality conflicts, and legacy disputes. On the other hand, affability alone will not make a meeting more effective. Each must be attended to as the group continues to evolve so that the dynamic exchange produces the desired outcomes—getting things done—and creates revitalization on the part of those participating in the meeting.

9. There are no agreed upon ground rules or working agreements.

Many meetings should have agreed-upon "working agreements" or ground rules for it to run smoothly. We have witnessed hundreds of meetings where people interrupt each other, talk over each other, conduct side bars throughout the meeting, are critical of each other if not downright mean. Having ground rules holds people accountable for productive meeting behavior (e.g., one person talks at a time; raise your hand to be acknowledged by the facilitator; use active listening).

10. Meetings are rarely evaluated for their effectiveness.

When was the last time you evaluated a meeting and saw the results of the evaluation? Most important meetings should be evaluated anonymously by the participants. It enables everyone to learn from the experience and prepares you to conduct better meetings in the future. This does not have to be a complex or time-consuming process. It can take five minutes, but what you will learn will be worth hundreds of people hours. A learning attitude is critical for effective meetings. Remember, if you ask for feedback, you better be ready for the results!

Some Thoughts about Facilitation

Overview

Many people think that because facilitation looks easy, it is easy. Others confuse the role of a facilitator with the role of a trainer. Facilitation is a complex and difficult process to master. The practice and craft of facilitation enables information to be exchanged in a way that builds connection, creativity, and involvement. The goals are to create a group process that enables the right kind of participation, to guide a group of people to a successful conclusion, and to work through complex discussions where differing points of view emerge and are needed. While remaining neutral is important, the art of facilitation includes knowing when to take a leadership role so that the needs of the group continue to be the focal point.

The Role of a Facilitator

While the actual word *facilitation* is to "make easy," the role of facilitation/facilitators can be defined as:

> "The facilitator's job is to *support everyone to do their best thinking and practice.* To do this, the facilitator encourages full participation, promotes mutual understanding, and cultivates shared responsibility. By supporting everyone to do their best thinking, a facilitator enables group members to search for inclusive solutions and build sustainable agreements."
>
> – Kaner (2007)

It is important to emphasize that the responsibility of the facilitator is to the group and its work rather than to the individuals within the group. The group gives the facilitator additional rights to accompany the increased responsibility. These rights depend on the decision made by the group, but often include the right to

- interrupt a speaker to ask if they are staying on subject, being concise, or repeating another person;

- be a participant and follow the same rules for speaking to the subject as everyone else;
- speak out of turn in order to assist the meeting process;
- make minor judgment calls on the agenda as the meeting progresses without asking permission of the group; and
- be an equal participant in the decision making (this is only appropriate if the facilitator is also a team member).

As the facilitator, your main responsibilities are to

- keep purposes clear;
- keep things moving;
- make sure everyone is involved; and
- make sure the group adheres to the "ground rules."

Facilitators are responsible for several things:

- **As logistics managers, facilitators understand the importance of creating the right environment for the process.** The room, the tables, the equipment, and other logistics give participants a sense about the meeting or process. Understanding where things are, how things will work, timeframes, and food breaks will increase participants' comfort levels and participation.

- **As role models, facilitators set the standard for the process.** They are open, setting the tone for a rich discussion, and at the same time set ground rules that enable people to operate well within the agreed-to boundaries. They need to listen and encourage everyone to contribute.

- **As leaders, facilitators need to continuously reinforce the value and need for each exercise and each discussion and continuously link the activity back to the overall goals.** In addition, facilitators need to address interference—those sidebars or other events that get in the way of activities and success.

- **As group behavior experts, facilitators must pay attention to what is going on with the group**. Facilitators need to stay focused and to observe. When necessary, it is important to "call it the way you see it" so that processes don't become burdensome, irrelevant, or stalled (e.g., "I notice that people are beginning to interrupt each other"; "We seem to be avoiding making a decision with this agenda item"; "I am not sure that we are listening to each other—can we practice active listening for a while?") Utilizing the tools and approaches in this book can also help to move things along.

- **As colleagues, facilitators need to create a relaxed environment**. Although many subjects can be difficult to discuss, that doesn't mean the climate has to be tension filled. Having fun should be part of what enables a good discussion.

Three Keys to Being a Facilitator

1. Be seen as credible to the participants.

Do you know what gets credibility in your group or organization? Is it experience? Age? Length of time in the organization? Degrees? Content expertise? "Nice" personality? If the facilitator doesn't match your group's expectations regarding credibility, it will be a difficult meeting. As a facilitator, you have about 30 minutes to establish your credibility with a group. When you introduce yourself, give a brief (one to two minutes) background of your experience and expertise. The participants want to know what your experience level is and how you can help them. If participants experience that the meeting is productive and that you are handling yourself well, your credibility bank account will go up.

2. Be neutral.

Swaying the group one way or another is an instant meeting process killer. Effective facilitators focus on the intended outcome only, using comments like: "Are we on the right track? Is this discussion helping us achieve the purpose of this meeting?" They stay away from judgmental comments like: "I really like that idea!" or "I'm not sure that would work." If participants sense the facilitator has a bias, there may be trouble. Stay neutral.

3. Understand the difference between a leader and facilitator.

Too often, leaders get trapped into thinking that they have to facilitate their own group's meetings. Leading and facilitating are two skills sets and roles. A facilitator should remain neutral, which is difficult for a leader to do. In addition, with a facilitator, leaders can fully participate.

Building Effectiveness as a Facilitator

The following are some ways to build your credibility and effectiveness:

1. **Get to know each participant's name** so that you can call on them by their name—it is important to people. Ask everyone to introduce themselves and then create a seating chart as they do "roll call."

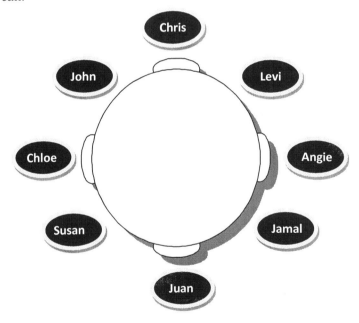

It is helpful to let people know that creating a seating chart so that you can learn their names is part of what you do. If you are not good with remembering names, then make sure you bring a sufficient number of name tags with you. Have participants put their first name only on the name tag and suggest that they write it in marker so that everyone can see it.

2. **Know the agenda, goals and history of the group.** It is rare to see a facilitator "parachute" into a meeting without doing his or her homework. You have to understand what the group wants to achieve and **why** it is important to them. Asking questions about the history of the problem and a little about the group members is helpful in understanding the complexity of the upcoming meeting.

   When participants realize that you have done your homework, again, your credibility is enhanced. Sometimes it is valuable to meet the key meeting attendees ahead of time.

3. **Create ground rules.** It is important to establish some ground rules up front, before you start the meeting. More importantly, you need to get each participant's agreement that they are appropriate. (Refer to Team Ground Rules on page 153). Basic ground rules like these will jump start the discussion about ground rules:

   - Talk one person at a time.
   - Raise your hand to be acknowledged.
   - Share air time with others.

   Post the ground rules on a flip chart in full view of everyone.

   Enforce the ground rules. Once you have agreement, make sure you hold people to them. Participants will be watching carefully to make sure you do this. If someone who is assertive or in a leadership position is "allowed" to break a ground rule, you will lose credibility fast. Gently remind the person about the ground rule and stick to it. (This is why it is important to get agreement up front, before the meeting starts. You want to avoid someone saying "I never liked that ground rule.")

4. **Pay attention.** If you are not familiar with the content of the discussion, this can be especially difficult to do. If participants realize that you are following the conversation and occasionally reflect back what you are hearing or summarizing viewpoints (e.g., "It seems as if we have agreement on who should attend the meeting, just not the number of people who should attend"), you will gain people's confidence.

5. **Paraphrase occasionally**. Another way to pay attention and build credibility is to paraphrase. Paraphrasing enables people to feel they are understood. They realize you are actually listening. This is a judgment call—don't get carried away with this. Use paraphrasing judiciously.

   It is especially helpful to paraphrase when there is conflict or strong differences of opinion. It tends to lower the intensity of the conflict (e.g., "Let me see if I understand, your greatest concern is that not enough people were involved in the survey. Is that right?").

6. **Invite differing opinions**. When someone speaks strongly on an issue, it is helpful to actively search for differing ideas (e.g., "Johanna, you seem to be saying that we shouldn't invite more people to the conference. Does anyone else have a different point of view?") By soliciting the ideas of others, you prevent a strong personality from dominating the discussion. Remember, your role is to keep people involved.

7. **Maintain eye contact with everyone**. Eye contact is important for many reasons. It establishes a rapport between the facilitator and participants that fosters trust. It allows the facilitator to read faces and know who is agitated, confused, or unhappy and should be called upon to speak. Eye contact helps keep everyone centered and in the "here and now" of the meeting.

8. **Suggest that participants raise their** hands to be acknowledged by the facilitator when the discussion gets fast and furious. This way you avoid interruptions. It is helpful to acknowledge that you see someone's hand with eye contact, a nod, or some gesture to let the person know you have seen them. This way they can relax and actually *listen* to the speaker, knowing they will be called on.

9. **Hold people to speaking for themselves** rather than making vague references to others. For example, discourage: "Some people say...," "We all know...," "They would not listen..." Even though this is difficult in the beginning, it will foster trust in the long run. Encourage "I" messages rather than "we" messages.

10. **Watch for "signals."** As a facilitator, one of the worst experiences you can have is seeing a participant (especially a powerful and respected one) go off on a tangent and take the meeting off track. We have found that there is a natural tendency for this to happen in most groups.

Get permission before the start of the meeting to "gently" interrupt participants to see if what they are talking about is helpful for the discussion. People who tend to go off on tangents usually signal that they are going to do this (e.g., "I don't mean to go off on a tangent, but...."; "I know this might be getting a little petty or detailed..."; or "This may be off track, but..."). When they send the verbal signal, intervene right then. Don't let them continue.

"Gently" remind them that we need to stay on track and focus on our purposes (e.g., "Thanks for the warning Al—I would appreciate it if we could stay on track.")

Another way to keep things moving is to use a **"Parking Lot"** to capture people's ideas and move ahead. (Please see the Toolbox section for a complete description of the Parking Lot tool).

Two things a facilitator should definitely pay attention to are:

- **The volume or loudness in a meeting**. When participants start to talk louder, something is going on (e.g., not feeling heard; conflict emerging). All you have to do is raise the process issue (e.g., "I've noticed that we are speaking loudly to each other"), and it often creates awareness for the group.

- **The number of interruptions in a conversation**. When people interrupt each other, the communication system has broken down. Raise the issue (e.g., "We are interrupting each other now and our ground rule states that one person at a time should talk.") Remember, loudness and interruptions are telltale signs of something going on. Don't diagnose (e.g., "I think that we are avoiding the issue or people are really being discourteous and disrespectful of one another.") Just state the observation, and the group will usually "rightsize" itself.

11. **Pause 10 seconds.** As a facilitator, you will often be in a position to pose a question to the group (e.g., "Are we on track?" "Where do you believe we are going with this discussion?" "We seem stuck, any suggestions?") After you pose a question, wait 10 seconds before you move on. Too often, a facilitator will ask a question and wait three to four seconds before moving on quickly. They let their personal anxiety hurry things along. Ask your question and wait 10 seconds for participants to think and respond.

12. **Make the group come up with a proposal** when enough discussion and process has occurred for a decision to be made. The facilitator can summarize what has been said and try to formulate a consensus proposal for the group to discuss, or the facilitator can stop the order of hands and ask someone in the group to come up with a proposal (e.g., "It seems that what I hear everyone saying is…" or "a rough consensus might be…"). Whenever the facilitator is "stuck," he or she should not hesitate to ask the group for help.

   Once a proposal is on the floor, ask who has serious objections to the proposal, and call on these people to speak. Once the serious objections are before the group, ask if someone can come up with a proposal that will resolve these concerns. Less serious concerns can be dealt with through wordsmithing the proposal and through friendly amendments.

13. **Be aware of time.** If you go over the proposed time limit, you will lose credibility. Don't let someone else define the time limits for you. You need to understand what needs to be accomplished and negotiate with the group leader or client how much time is necessary to fulfill the purpose.

   If you are given one hour to facilitate a discussion about a particular topic, use a timer to signal when 30 minutes is up ("half-time"). Check with the group on how things are progressing. Again, set the timer for 20 minutes, which will give you 10 minutes to go. Don't be surprised by the time limit.

If you have 10 minutes to go and it is clear that you need more time, bring it to the group's attention (e.g., "I can see that we are making progress, but we are up against the clock. Can we add an additional 15 minutes to this part of the agenda?"). Have the group decide what to do with the time issue—just make sure you give them fair warning.

14. **Communicate commitments/actions/next steps.** It is important that before participants leave you help create a clear sense of closure for the meeting. The last 10 minutes of a meeting can get sloppy with too many loose ends. To avoid this,

   - identify any next steps that have been agreed to;
   - ensure that the minutes or flip chart information will be distributed in a timely manner and by whom;
   - review any Parking Lot issues.

   If there are clear actions that have been decided, review these with the group and make sure everyone understands the implications (e.g., what support will people need to complete their actions? How will they keep others informed? When will the action or steps be completed?). Bottom line: your job is to make sure that things get tied up well.

15. **Decide "how to decide" up front.** It is important that everyone understand and agree to the decision rules before the meeting begins. The last thing you want is to get to a decision point in a meeting and find out there is confusion. Some suggestions about decision making in groups include the following:

   - **Stay away from the word *consensus*.** This is a word that is used promiscuously and one that few agree on the definition. If you are going to use *consensus*, make sure you define it up front for everyone and get their agreement on the definition. This will not be easy, but it is worth the extra effort. Our definition:

     "Consensus has been reached when everyone agrees that the process has been fair and transparent, people feel heard, good information was used to make the final decision, and people are willing to support (not necessarily be happy with) the final decision."

The LUIS Formula is a helpful model for understanding consensus:

> **L** = I *like* the decision.
> **U** = I *understand* the decision.
> **I** = I was *involved* in making the decision.
> **S** = I will *support* the decision.

- **The 85/15 Rule.** When decision time comes, the group agrees, up front, that if 85 percent of the meeting participants/group members agree on a decision, it is enough to pass. This alleviates the "tyranny of the minority" where two or three people out of 12 or 15 people can hold a decision hostage.

- **Super majority.** It takes a two-thirds vote in the senate to pass new legislation, so it is a constructive threshold.

- **Simple majority (51/49 vote for a decision).** Stay away from these kinds of votes. They will come back to haunt you in the end, especially if you have a lot of them. You won't be able to implement very many simple majority decisions.

Summary

One of the most important things a facilitator needs to remember is to stay focused on the purposes of the meeting. Your goal is not to lead the group or fix people. If you spend time with a group, you will see "problems" that need to be fixed. This is not your role. Focus on purposes, ground rules, involving people, and outcomes.

The Highly Effective Meeting Profile[*]

Instructions

This survey is designed to enable you to assess your meeting effectiveness over time; it is **not** helpful in evaluating a one-time meeting or conference. Therefore, it is appropriate to use this survey only with intact and ongoing groups or teams that meet on a regular basis (e.g., once a week).

On the following pages, you will find 50 statements relating to effective meetings. If you *mostly agree* (if the statement is true more than 75 percent of the time) that a particular statement represents how your meetings actually function, please mark an X in the corresponding box on the answer sheet.

For example, if you *mostly agree* that Statement #6 ("Participants understand how decisions will be made *before* we make an important decision") accurately reflects how your group operates, mark an X in the #6 box on the answer sheet. If you *do not* mostly agree with a statement, please leave the corresponding box blank.

Please try to respond to all the statements. If you are uncertain about a particular statement, answer it as best you can and move on to the next statement. Because of the large number of statements, no single item will change the overall picture.

It is important to remember that this is a learning tool, not a vehicle for criticism. The statements in this survey represent the best of what a meeting can be. Even though it is informal in nature, the standards are very rigorous. We recognize that it is difficult to produce consistently effective meetings. Therefore, use the profile to diagnose what works and what needs improvement in your ongoing meetings; don't use the survey results to beat yourself up.

---

[*] Sanaghan, Goldstein & Conway. Amherst, MA: HRD Press, Inc. (2003).

For best results, the responses to this survey need to be *anonymous.* This will enhance the likelihood of receiving honest information from participants.

A final note: We call this a "common sense survey" because it is meant to be user friendly. This is *not* a complex, validated instrument. We created this profile after observing thousands of meetings that ranged from poorly designed and nonproductive to highly creative, engaging, and results oriented. The survey will help you diagnose the effectiveness of your meetings and identify practical ways to improve them.

Appendix

Meeting Effectiveness Profile Diagnostic Statements

1. Overall, the quality of our decision making is good.

2. Participants come well-prepared to our meetings.

3. People feel free to discuss sensitive issues in our meetings.

4. We have an agenda for our meetings.

5. Real participation of all group members is encouraged in our meetings.

6. Participants understand how decisions will be made *before* we make an important decision (e.g., consensus, simple majority, the leader has the final say).

7. Our agenda has a sense of priority to it. We spend most of our time on the most important items.

8. There is a high level of trust between participants in our meetings.

9. We take time to review the agenda at the beginning of our meetings.

10. I feel involved in what's going on during our meetings.

11. People generally feel that they can influence the decisions made in this group.

12. We establish accountability by reviewing action items from the previous meeting to determine their status and communicate progress.

13. Conflict is dealt with effectively in our meetings.

14. We usually have mechanisms for capturing or recording the essence of what takes place during our meetings (e.g., action items, agreements).

15. Other members solicit my opinions and participation during our meetings.

16. We usually have an agreed-upon set of criteria to help us evaluate different alternatives before we make an important decision.

17. Before our meetings end, we review what has been agreed to regarding action items and next steps.

18. People tend to be open to the ideas of others in our meetings.

19. We usually have someone who acts as a facilitator to keep things moving and to help people stay involved during our meetings.

20. The quality of our discussions is high (e.g., issues are examined in depth, problems are addressed and not skirted).

21. We review outcomes to track the quality of the important decisions we have made.

22. Our meetings are a valuable use of my time because we deal with important content.

23. People feel comfortable challenging the ideas and comments of others in our meetings.

24. Minutes or a record of our meetings are distributed to participants in a timely manner following the meeting.

25. We try different ways to ensure that people get an opportunity to participate (e.g., use brainstorming, mind mapping, breaking into small groups to discuss a problem).

26. We use a variety of decision-making tools (e.g., multivoting, Nominal Group Technique) in our meetings.

27. If a participant goes off track, they are redirected appropriately.

28. There are no personal attacks during our meetings.

29. All relevant materials needed for our meetings (e.g., reports, graphs, and financial statements) are distributed in advance of the meeting and enable us to read and digest the information before we meet.

30. Different ideas and perspectives are often explored in our meetings.

31. The processes we use to arrive at a decision are effective.

32. Commitments made at our meetings are followed up on and not forgotten.

33. People really listen to each other during our meetings.

34. If we get stuck on a particular item, we have a process that allows us to capture the item (e.g., "Grass Catcher," "Parking Lot") and continue with our meeting.

35. There is appropriate input from regular participants in creating our agendas.

36. When making important decisions, we usually have a structured approach that everyone understands.

37. Unfinished business from a previous meeting is dealt with at the next meeting.

38. We periodically use part of our meeting to celebrate good news and share successes.

39. We adhere to an agreed-upon set of "ground rules" or working agreements to enhance the effectiveness of our meetings (e.g., only one person talks at a time, no sidebars, start and end the meeting on time).

40. During our meetings, people are generally focused on the task at hand (e.g., minimal sidebars; no passing notes, reading e-mails, or writing a novel!).

41. When appropriate, we use facts, relevant information, and research to influence and inform our decision making.

42. We periodically evaluate the effectiveness of our meetings.

43. Other members in this group value my opinion.

44. We generally start and end our meetings on time.

45. Participation is usually energetic and stimulating.

46. We usually tap the resources and talents of those in attendance when it comes to making decisions (e.g., different perspectives, expertise, thinking styles).

47. We seek closure on agenda items—things are not left hanging.

48. For the most part, there are no hidden agendas in our meetings (e.g., people vying for power, sabotaging other participants).

49. If someone is absent, a participant in the meeting takes responsibility for informing the member about what took place.

50. People feel that our meetings are worthwhile because their participation makes a difference in the outcomes, decisions, and results.

Meeting Effectiveness Profile Answer Sheet

Mark an X in each box only if you mostly agree with the corresponding statement on the previous pages.

1. ☐	2. ☐	3. ☐	4. ☐	5. ☐
6. ☐	7. ☐	8. ☐	9. ☐	10. ☐
11. ☐	12. ☐	13. ☐	14. ☐	15. ☐
16. ☐	17. ☐	18. ☐	19. ☐	20. ☐
21. ☐	22. ☐	23. ☐	24. ☐	25. ☐
26. ☐	27. ☐	28. ☐	29. ☐	30. ☐
31. ☐	32. ☐	33. ☐	34. ☐	35. ☐
36. ☐	37. ☐	38. ☐	39. ☐	40. ☐
41. ☐	42. ☐	43. ☐	44. ☐	45. ☐
46. ☐	47. ☐	48. ☐	49. ☐	50. ☐

When completed, follow the directions on the Scoring Sheet.

Scoring the Survey: The Categories

In our extensive research and observations of thousands of meetings over the past 20 years, we have found five key categories or elements of effective meetings:

1. Effective *decision-making* processes
2. A *results orientation* (a focus on accomplishing things in a meeting)
3. Positive *group climate*
4. Basic *procedures and protocols*
5. Real *participation and engagement*

All five of these categories need to be addressed if you are going to produce highly effective meetings. The hundreds of books and articles that have been written about meetings focus on one, two, or maybe three categories. This is not enough to have truly effective meetings. As a group leader, facilitator, or consultant, you have to be able to diagnose each element and improve each category to achieve excellence.

If you have a high results orientation, but poor decision-making processes, you will continue to run into walls. If you have very good procedures and protocols in place but poor group climate, you will never tap the talent and resources of the group. The categories in this profile are usually not thought about in a disciplined way. In too many cases, it is assumed that if we are smart people with the right agenda, magical things will happen. Our experience has demonstrated this is not reality in most cases.

In the survey of 50 statements, the categories described below are the subject of 10 statements each:

A. **Decision Making**: Statements 1, 6, 11, 16, 21, 26, 31, 36, 41, and 46 cover Decision Making. The quality of a group's decision-making ability defines its real value to the organization. A group of really smart people can make poor decisions without effective group practices. High-performing groups consistently make good decisions. This category assesses your decision-making processes and determines their current effectiveness.

B. **Results Orientation**: Statements 2, 7, 12, 17, 22, 27, 32, 37, 42, and 47 cover Results Orientation. Many meetings are opportunities for participants to gab, defer decisions, talk an issue to death, or listen to blowhards. Effective groups meet to accomplish things. You can have all the procedures and protocols in place and even have positive group climate and not achieve anything meaningful. This category assesses orientation to action, sense of priority, and commitment to produce results. Without a results focus, very little else matters.

C. **Group Climate**: Statements 3, 8, 13, 18, 23, 28, 33, 38, 43, and 48 cover Group Climate. This is one area that rarely gets discussed when talking about meeting effectiveness. You can have highly driven, very smart, responsible people in a meeting, but if the group's climate is poor, little will be accomplished. It will take courage and discipline to tackle this category. We believe it may be the most important element of all. Relationships do matter because you achieve results through people. This category will give you a snapshot of how people feel about the meeting interaction and relationships among participants.

D. **Procedures and Protocols**: Statements 4, 9, 14, 19, 24, 29, 34, 39, 44, and 49 cover Procedures and Protocols. Excellent meetings have clear processes and protocols in place to ensure effective meeting practices and outcomes. These are the "nuts and bolts" of a good meeting and are essential to the success of any meeting. By reviewing these elements, you can build the appropriate structures to support your meetings.

E. **Participation and Engagement**: Statements 5, 10, 15, 20, 25, 30, 35, 40, 45, and 50 cover Participation and Engagement. The reason you bring people together is to tap their ideas, imagination, and inspiration. Too often, this does not happen. Real participation does not just happen by luck or by putting a group of smart people together. It must be planned for and designed into the meeting. This category enables you to look at different techniques to ensure full participation by everyone in attendance at a meeting. Don't leave it to chance.

How to Score the Survey

1. When you receive each group member's **anonymous** Answer Sheet, place their scores in the appropriate boxes. Use the Scoring Sheet.

2. After you enter each participant's score, add up all the totals.

3. After you have the group totals for each category, divide by the number of survey participants. For example, if there were **eight** survey participants, divide by 8 to get the average score for each category (if you have six participants, divide each total by 6, etc.).

   A. Decision Making = 30 votes ÷ 8 = 3.8
   B. Results Orientation = 51 votes ÷ 8 = 6.4
   C. Group Climate = 25 votes ÷ 8 = 3.1
   D. Procedures and Protocols = 64 votes ÷ 8 = 8.0
   E. Participation and Engagement = 20 votes ÷ 8 = 2.5

   The graph for this group would look like this:

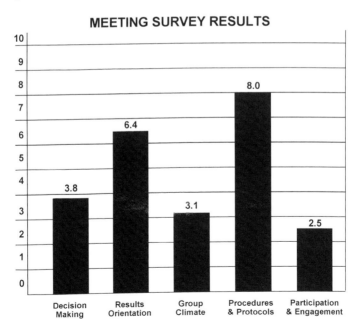

As you can quickly see, this group is very strong in the Procedures and Protocols category and strong in the Results Orientation category. Obviously, they need to work on their Decision Making, Group Climate, and Participation and Engagement.

An effective meeting environment is evidenced when all scores are in the 6 to 8 range. A score below 5 in a category indicates a need to focus on improving that area. Scores below 3 indicate a serious problem and a need for significant effort to improve that area.

Meeting Effectiveness Profile Scoring Sheet

You can graph your group's distribution by plotting the responses from the answer sheet on the form below. Take the averages from the answer sheet, draw a line on each box at the appropriate level, and shade the column up to that point.

	Decision Making	Results Orientation	Group Climate	Procedures & Protocols	Participation & Engagement
10					
9					
8					
7					
6					
5					
4					
3					
2					
1					

Diagnosis and Item Analysis

After you have tabulated the results of your group and created a graph, you will have a clear picture of the strengths and weaknesses of your group meetings. In our example, it is obvious that this particular group is strong in the areas of (B) Results Orientation (6.4) and (D) Procedures and Protocols (8.0), but needs to improve in three areas: (A) Decision Making (3.8); (C) Group Climate (3.1); and (E) Participation and Engagement (2.5).

In the next few pages, we have organized the 50 statements from the profile into the five categories from the survey (i.e., Decision Making, Results Orientation, Group Climate, Procedures and Protocols, and Participation and Engagement). We have found it helpful to do an item analysis of each category in order to clearly understand how partici-pants perceive and experience your meetings.

Before you proceed to the Solutions section, it is important to figure out exactly where the problems really lie. For example:

A. In the **Decision Making** category, you need to see how many peo-ple scored a particular statement from that category. Statement #11—People generally feel that they can influence the decisions made in this group—might have scored rather high from group members (e.g., 6 out of 8), but statement #41—When appropriate, we use facts, relevant information, and research to influence and inform our decision making—might have scored very low (e.g., 1 out of 8). You want to know what the real problems are before you try to solve them or apply some of our solutions.

B. In the **Group Climate** category, you might have a high score on statement #8—There is a high level of trust between participants in our meetings—but a very low score for statement #13—Con-flict is dealt with effectively in our meetings. These two statements reveal two very different problems.

247

C. In the **Participation and Engagement** section, statement #5—Real participation of all group members is encouraged in our meetings—might receive relatively high scores, but statement #40—During our meetings, people are generally focused on the task at hand—might receive low scores.

Bottom line, you want to clearly establish the real problems before you start to solve them. This takes extra effort, but will reap many rewards. The survey gives you a general "X-ray" of the group's meeting effectiveness; item analysis gives you an "MRI." Take the time—it's worth it.

Each category has its own challenges when you try to improve your meeting effectiveness. Procedures and Protocols is the easiest category to improve upon and you can see real progress rather quickly if you focus on that area. Improving the categories of Decision Making, Results Orientation, and Participation and Engagement will take time, effort, and discipline. Try to improve one area at a time instead of tackling all three. This way you will experience some early success and create the momentum necessary for positive change.

The last category, Group Climate, will be the most difficult to improve because it deals with people's interactions, issues of trust, and even feelings. You can have high marks in the other four areas, but low scores in this category will have a negative impact on the effectiveness of your meetings, guaranteed.

Decision Making

1. Overall, the quality of our decision making is good.

6. Participants understand how the decisions will be made *before* we make an important decision (e.g., consensus, simple majority, the leader has the final say).

11. People generally feel that they can influence the decisions made in this group.

16. We usually have an agreed-upon set of criteria to help us evaluate different alternatives before we make an important decision.

21. We review outcomes to track the quality of the important decisions we have made.

26. We use a variety of decision-making tools (e.g., multivoting, Nominal Group Technique) in our meetings.

31. The processes we use to arrive at a decision are effective.

36. When making important decisions, we usually have a structured approach that everyone understands.

41. When appropriate, we use facts, relevant information, and research to influence and inform our decision making.

46. We usually tap the resources and talents of those in attendance when it comes to making decisions (e.g., different perspectives, expertise, thinking styles).

Results Orientation

2. Participants come well-prepared to our meetings.

7. Our agenda has a sense of priority to it. We spend most of our time on the most important items.

12. We establish accountability by reviewing action items from the previous meeting to determine their status and communicate progress.

17. Before our meetings end, we review what has been agreed to regarding action items and next steps.

22. Our meetings are a valuable use of my time because we deal with important content.

27. If participants go off track, they are redirected appropriately.

32. Commitments made at our meetings are followed up on and not forgotten.

37. Unfinished business from a previous meeting is dealt with at the next meeting.

42. We periodically evaluate the effectiveness of our meetings.

47. We seek closure on agenda items—things are not left hanging.

Group Climate

3. People feel free to discuss sensitive issues in our meetings.

8. There is a high level of trust between participants in our meetings.

13. Conflict is dealt with effectively in our meetings.

18. People tend to be open to the ideas of others in our meetings.

23. People feel comfortable challenging the ideas and comments of others in our meetings.

28. There are no personal attacks during our meetings.

33. People really listen to each other during our meetings.

38. We periodically use part of our meeting to celebrate good news and share successes.

43. Other members in this group value my opinion.

48. For the most part, there are no hidden agendas in our meetings (e.g., people vying for power, sabotaging other participants).

Procedures and Protocols

4. We have an agenda for our meetings

9. We take time to review the agenda at the beginning of our meetings.

14. We usually have mechanisms for capturing or recording the essence of what takes place during our meetings (e.g., action items, agreements).

19. We usually have someone who acts as a facilitator to keep things moving and to help people stay involved during our meetings.

24. Minutes or a record of our meetings are distributed to participants in a timely manner following the meeting.

29. All relevant materials needed for our meetings (e.g., reports, graphs, financial statements) are distributed in advance of the meeting to enable us to read and digest the information before we meet.

34. If we get stuck on a particular item, we have a process that allows us to capture the item (e.g., "Grass Catcher," "Parking Lot") and continue with our meeting.

39. We adhere to an agreed-upon set of "ground rules" or working agreements to enhance the effectiveness of our meetings (e.g., only one person talks at a time, no sidebars, start and end the meeting on time).

44. We generally start and end our meetings on time.

49. If someone is absent, a participant in the meeting takes responsibility for informing the member about what took place.

Participation and Engagement

5. Real participation of all group members is encouraged in our meetings.

10. I feel involved in what's going on during our meetings.

15. Other members solicit my opinions and participation during our meetings.

20. The quality of our discussions is high (e.g., issues are examined in depth, problems are addressed and not skirted).

25. We try different ways to ensure that people get an opportunity to participate (e.g., use brainstorming, mind mapping, breaking into small groups to discuss a problem).

30. Different ideas and perspectives are often explored in our meetings.

35. There is appropriate input from regular participants in creating our agendas.

40. During our meetings, people are generally focused on the task at hand (e.g., minimal sidebars; no passing notes, reading e-mails, or writing a novel!).

45. Participation is usually energetic and stimulating.

50. People feel that our meetings are worthwhile because their participation makes a difference in the outcomes, decisions, and results.

27 Ways to Improve Your Meetings

1. Skip Monday morning meetings—they are usually not a good idea.

About 80 percent of the organizations we have worked with have Monday morning meetings to "kick off" the week. This is especially true at the senior level. This idea looks good on paper but is often detrimental in practice.

We suggest you have a Monday *afternoon* "kick off" meeting or wait until Tuesday morning. Some reasons why:

1) While attending a Monday morning meeting, people psychologically are thinking about their staff, wondering what's going on in their department/division, still thinking about the weekend, worrying about the problems that await them.

2) Let people have Monday morning to check in with their people, problem solve, and get things moving in their units. This way when they come to the Monday afternoon meeting, they will be psychologically connected to what is going on.

3) Waiting until Monday afternoon gives people extra time to prepare for the "kick off" meeting. They can review the necessary information *before* they come to the meeting and do some thinking so that they are prepared for the meeting.

4) There will be less stress about the meeting because the sense of urgency that accompanies the usual Monday morning meeting will be neutralized.

2. Check people's time commitments before you begin your meeting.

This is an important thing to do, especially when you have a diverse group of people throughout the organization attending a meeting or you have a combination of insiders and outsiders (e.g., customers, community members, vendors) attending your meeting.

Doing this helps with two things:

1) It alerts you to who will be leaving before the official time of the meeting. You might have to adjust your agenda to make sure someone who has to leave early is utilized appropriately. For example: there might be a specific agenda item that an "early leaver" is an expert about and you want to use their expertise. Just let participants know what you are thinking.

   "Mary has to leave at 1:30 and I would like to suggest we move up the agenda item on the technology infrastructure so that we can get her advice before she has to leave. Is that okay with folks?" Get approval and keep on moving.

2) Whenever a person leaves a meeting, it changes the group dynamics. It can either add or detract the energy and focus of the meeting. For example: If a senior-level person leaves early, participants might psychologically relax when the leader leaves *or* feel like the meeting is less important after the leader leaves. You need to be prepared for both scenarios and remind participants that they still have important work to do and that you expect full participation.

3. Ground rules are essential.

For any regular meeting, it is important to have some working agreements or ground rules to which participants are committed. Make sure there is agreement on the ground rules *before* beginning the meeting.

Our favorite ground rule is "one person speaks at a time." This helps eliminate all the aggravating sidebars that take place in most meetings that take the energy and focus away from the discussion. If you see more than one person talking during a meeting, gently remind people of the ground rule. Don't single anyone out (e.g., "Pat, can you stop talking while Barbara is explaining the new budget?"). Just state the ground rule as a reminder to everyone. Do it as soon as it occurs so that you nip it in the bud, especially if someone senior is the guilty party. If participants see the facilitator let the senior leader violate the ground rule, you don't have a ground rule any more.

Another effective ground rule is "start and end on time." This helps communicate that everyone's time is valuable and gives the meeting leader/facilitator permission to begin the meeting on time, even if someone is missing. It also holds the leader/facilitator accountable for ending on time, so be careful what you wish for!

Use whatever ground rules you believe will help you have an effective meeting. Pay attention to both **task** (e.g., start and end on time, distribute agenda before meeting) and the **process** (e.g., practice active listening, one person talks at a time) elements of meetings.

The key thing to remember is that meeting participants need to agree with the ground rules before you begin the meeting. It is hard to impose ground rules halfway into the meeting ("Why don't we now agree to raise our hands and be acknowledged by the facilitator").

4. **Poker chips and paper clips.**

This is a technique we have used several times and is very effective with highly verbal, dominating, or contentious meeting participants.

Before the meeting, distribute 5 to 10 poker chips or paper clips to everyone. Communicate the following to participants: "Every time you speak, please put one of your poker chips in the center of the table. For every three minutes you speak, it will cost you another poker chip. After all your poker chips are spent, you can no longer *verbally* participate in the meeting, just listen to others and observe. This prevents one person from monopolizing the conversation."

Obviously, this technique will not work if people don't agree with it. It will take the senior leader to sanction the technique. They must be willing to give legitimacy to trying this powerful technique.

When utilizing this technique, several things will happen:

1) The overly verbal participants will spend their poker chips quickly.

2) Sometimes the "verbals" will actually think before they speak because their participation costs them something.

3) The quieter participants will have most of the chips and begin participating more. This is what you want to happen.

5. Use a timer.

This is a technique that can work very well but must be used judiciously. The goal should be to make people aware of time, not create a false sense of urgency during the meeting. For example, let's say there is an allotted 30 minutes for discussion on a specific topic. Set the timer to go off in 15 minutes. This "half time" reminder will let people know how much time is left and usually focuses participants' attention quickly.

Kitchen timers are great because they have a clear signal when they go off.

6. To lead or facilitate?

We often get asked this question by leaders: "Should I facilitate the meeting or be a participant in my meeting?" We have found that trying to be the leader and the facilitator is fraught with danger (well, maybe not danger, but it's not a good idea.)

Leaders often have a vested interest in the decisions that will be made during a meeting. Facilitators should never have an interest in what the final decision will be. Their role is to move the group toward a good decision *and be neutral.*

Often, a leader cannot be neutral about where a decision is going. Everyone knows this and will wait until the leader signals what he or she believes the decision should be.

We suggest the leader appoint or assign someone to be the facilitator who has no vested interest in the outcome of the meeting and participate as the leader.

7. Watch out for two signals that your meeting is in trouble!

Often, when there is an important or hot topic being discussed in a meeting, participants will start talking fast and furiously. As a facilitator, you need to pay attention to two things:

- **Interruptions:** When more than one person is talking and people are talking over each other, it is a sign that the communication process has broken down. Participants cannot pay attention to two conversations, even if they think they can.

  As the facilitator of the meeting, all you have to do is bring to conscious attention the fact that people are interrupting each other and things will almost always quiet down. For example, "I notice that we have more than one person talking at a time" will suffice.

- **Volume:** When you notice that people are talking louder during a meeting, it is important to gently intervene. When people talk louder, it usually means they *don't feel heard*. Once again, just state what you see: "I notice that some of us are speaking more loudly." Just state this *without judgment* and it will bring it to participants' attention and usually quiet things down.

8. One minute of silence.

This is a great technique to use when things are moving too fast or the group has run out of ideas. Just suggest that participants take one minute to think about what is being discussed silently.

This will either slow things down when they are moving too fast or, with a group that has run out of ideas, it can create the psychological space to generate new ideas and spark a creative discussion.

It can also be a useful technique when a group is experiencing some conflict or tempers are rising. One minute of silence can create the space for something new to evolve (e.g., more insight, empathy, cooling down).

9. Confirm, confirm, confirm!

We have found that somewhere between 20 to 30 percent of meetings are cancelled or postponed. It is always a good idea to have a "rain date" for a meeting; this way you have a fallback position.

Make sure to double check and confirm the time and place for a meeting you will be attending so that you don't waste your time traveling to a meeting that was cancelled the day before.

10. Start with the most important agenda item first.

Many of us have gotten into the habit of covering trivial items at the beginning of our meetings. There are two primary reasons for this:

1) It allows the latecomers to miss the "little stuff" and be there when the real meeting occurs. This also encourages lateness because people think, "heck, the first 10 minutes aren't important anyway."

2) It is *supposed* to create some "positive momentum." The thinking behind this is if we knock off a few items early in the meetings, people will feel like they have accomplished something. This is not true.

Starting with the most important agenda item first does several things:

a) It conveys respect for those participants who arrived on time.

b) It discourages the latecomers from coming late because "juicy" stuff happens early.

c) You use your meeting time more effectively and strategically because the priority stuff is dealt with early when people are more alert. In the second half of a meeting, people can feel rushed or may have "checked out" because they are thinking about the next meeting they have to attend.

11. The One-Third – One-Third – One-Third Rule.

Because of their learning style, many people like to receive pertinent meeting information before the meeting. Theoretically, they want to read the information ahead of time so that they can come prepared to the meeting. Although this is a wonderful intention, the meeting facilitator or leader should expect the following:

> One-third of the meeting participants will actually read the material carefully; one-third will misplace or say they never received the material; one-third will be reading the material on the way to the meeting!

The reason we bring this up: do not assume everyone is fully prepared for your meeting. Instead, have a general discussion about the important elements in the meeting materials, highlight these, capture them on a whiteboard or a flip chart, and continue the meeting.

This way everyone is on board, and no one has to admit they didn't have a chance to read the information prior to the meeting.

12. Round tables are usually best.

Whenever possible, use round tables for your meetings. They help encourage dialogue and discussion and convey the feeling that we are all on the same level. There are no "power" positions with round tables; whereas, with rectangular tables, the ends of the table are where the "power" people sit.

13. With intense meetings, use the right layout.

Although we usually like round tables for our meetings so that everyone can easily see each other, there are times when it is *not* a good idea.

When there is an intense conflict about a topic, or a strong disagreement about a decision being made or when certain people have problems with each other, it is more effective to have the group sit in a semicircle facing a white board or flip charts rather than face each other.

This way the intensity can be managed by the facilitator and directed to the task at hand. Facing the wall and not each other diffuses the energy dramatically.

14. Get rid of extra chairs.

If you are facilitating a meeting for 12 people and there are 20 chairs in the room, get rid of the empty chairs if you can. Put them in a hallway, stack them up, or put them in the back of the room.

Empty chairs are distracting: people sometimes wonder who is missing from the meeting or who "should" be attending. Unconsciously it conveys that the meeting can't be that important because the room is not filled.

15. The "strategic" use of time.

It is helpful to start your meetings on the quarter or half hour (e.g., 11:15, 12:30, 1:45). It encourages punctuality. Avoid the hour (11:00, 3:00) starting time because if people come at 11:07, they can feel like they are "almost on time."

- Most people are not very good at the allotment of time for agenda items. They "guesstimate" and are usually wrong. Remember, Analytics and Practicals *love short meetings*. They will often allot 5 or 10 minutes for an agenda item that needs much more time. This is not a criticism, simply a factor to consider.

- For important agenda items, add an additional 15 minutes to your original estimate. That way if things are going well, you have some wiggle room. If you finish early, you will look like a genius.

- People can only pay attention for about 45 minutes, and that's *if they are interested* in the topic! It is a good idea to take short (5-minute) stretch breaks every hour or so. This will allow people to take care of themselves, create more energy, and even spark some creative ideas when people return.

Make sure you communicate the time limit before you take the stretch break. Get agreement on how long the stretch break should be (never more than 10 minutes).

It is helpful to remind people that if the stretch breaks take longer, the overall meeting will be longer.

16. "Working" lunch = a bad idea.

We don't like working lunches, but highly task-orientated people seem to love them. They assume they can "kill two birds with one stone" by eating and working through lunch. It is rarely a good idea.

A working lunch is usually an indication that the agenda was way too ambitious or the discussions way too long. It can get real ugly when people are talking and chewing, waving a sandwich for emphasis, spilling their drinks, dribbling, and wiping their mouths.

Give people 20 minutes to eat their food in a civilized manner. Then get back to the meeting. Have the food delivered in the room so that people stay there. If they have to go someplace else for lunch, they will migrate all over the place.

17. We hate latecomers!

We realize when people come late to meetings they often have legitimate excuses/reasons (e.g., stuck in traffic, train delayed, boss called a meeting at the last minute).

Too often, we all suffer from *perpetual* latecomers. The following are some suggestions:

- Make sure you arrange the room so that latecomers can enter from the back of the room and slip in quietly.

- Make sure you have an agenda and all appropriate materials for latecomers so that they don't fumble around and ask for help.

- Try mightily *not* to review all that has been accomplished so far in the meeting. That's what minutes are for. Obviously, if the boss comes late, it would be smart to get him or her up to speed, but avoid it if you can.

- With important meetings, some organizations have a "gate-keeper" whose job is to bridge latecomers into the meeting. Offline or out of the room, they review what has taken place so far and where the group is currently. They do this *quietly*.

- Lastly, and this is a little sneaky but fun, you can establish a protocol that latecomers (*not the legitimate ones*) take the meeting minutes. You will be amazed how motivating this can be.

18. Switch seats periodically.

In a long meeting (one-half to one day), encourage participants to switch where they sit once or twice in the meeting. This should occur after a break or after lunch. This helps create more energy in the group, give people a different perspective, and make sure the same people are not sitting together all day.

19. Get stuck... move on and come back.

During a meeting, if your group gets "stuck" on a particular agenda item, suggest moving ahead to the next agenda item. Let participants know that you will return to the difficult item (*this is essential*) after you have finished the next one.

Doing this gives participants a psychological break, shifts their thinking and may create the opportunity to gain insight and perspective about the challenging issue. It can also create the positive momentum to tackle the difficult item after successfully accomplishing the easier one.

20. State the agenda items as questions.

This is a traditional technique that works quite well. Instead of listing the items on the agenda as topics (e.g., onboarding, organizational morale, core process problems), state them as questions. For example, "How can we further improve our organization's climate?" "How can we create the best onboarding process for our incoming interns?" "What about our core process is working and what is not?"

Stating the agenda items as questions can stimulate thinking and creativity because most of us like the challenge of a question and will want to answer it!

21. Natural endings.

When you schedule an ongoing meeting (e.g., a group that meets weekly), it is helpful to hold your meetings about an hour before lunch time or an hour before the end of the day. People will get hungry and want to move things forward or want to get home. Natural endings can be great motivators for staying on track and on time.

22. Review where you have been and where you are going.

If you are participating in a group that has a series of meetings over time (e.g., task force, committee), it is helpful to review where you have been as a group. For example, "The last time we were together, we read the organizational climate survey, brainstormed some ideas, and prioritized the best ones. Today we are going to create action plans to move the best ideas forward and provide feedback for each other about our action plans. The goal at the end of the meeting is to have four operational plans that will be implemented over the next three months."

23. Make time for advocacy.

Before an *important* decision is to be made in a meeting, create the opportunity for each participant to state their position *and* the thinking behind their position. Don't allow any debate or questions. Each person has 1 to 2 minutes to say what they need to say. After the "advocacy" round, have participants vote anonymously on the best decision. This way, no one can unduly influence others in the final decision.

24. Two techniques that encourage participation.

1) **Do a think/pair/share:** The meeting leader/facilitator asks the group a focus question regarding the agenda item (e.g., "How can we have a reward and recognition program that doesn't cost more money?" or "What can we do to improve customer service?").

Ask each meeting participant to **think** of some strategies and ideas and write them down on a piece of paper. Give them two minutes to do this. Then ask them to **pair** up with the person sitting next to them and *share* their ideas. Give them two to three minutes for this. Then ask the participants to **share** their best ideas with the entire group.

The meeting facilitator should take **one** idea from each group, write it in full view of everyone on a flip chart, and go around as many times as necessary. The reason you take **one** idea from each pair is that you want everyone to feel like they have added something of value to the conversation. If you have six "pairs" in a meeting and take *all* the ideas from the first and second pair, there is a good chance the other pairs will not have anything to contribute because the first two groups will have shared all the good ideas. You want to avoid this.

2) **Index cards:** With this technique, the meeting facilitator hands out several index cards to each meeting participant. Again ask the group a relevant focus question and ask them to write their answers on the available index cards. Let them know there are plenty more index cards if they need them and that *legibility* is important. No names should be attached to an index card.

Give them about five minutes to write down their answers and have them hand them into the meeting facilitator. The facilitator then writes down the suggestions on a flip chart. Ask someone to help you write down the ideas so that the meeting moves quickly.

After the list of ideas is written, the group can review each item and discuss it. If you are trying to reach a decision about the suggested ideas, you can use the Las Vegas Voting or the Nominal Group Technique located in the Toolbox section.

Using index cards does several things:

- It **neutralizes** the most verbal participants. Instead of blabbing away off the top of their heads, they have to slow down and **think** about the question or problem. You will find the suggestions will be more thoughtful and considered using this technique.

- It **involves** the quieter or more shy meeting participants. Those individuals who might be reluctant to participate verbally will feel much more comfortable writing their ideas down.

- It also neutralizes power or bias in the meeting discussion. When people don't know who said what, each idea rises and falls on its own merit. If everyone knows what ideas the leader is proposing, it is easy to agree how "brilliant" they are.

This is a very simple technique with lots of benefits.

25. Review group agreements before people leave.

One of the things that drives people crazy and promotes ineffective meetings is poor wrap-up at the end of the meeting. You can have an exciting, energizing, productive meeting and blow it all away in the last 10 to 15 minutes of the meeting.

You have to be very disciplined about *summarizing* the decisions made and next steps before the end of the meeting. Two things to remember:

1) People will tend to resist this because it holds them accountable and psychologically they are already out the door.

2) You have to build in time in the agenda to do this or it won't happen.

If you have a one-hour meeting, you need to take the last 10 minutes to clarify what has been agreed to, and to review responsible next steps and who's accountable, specific assignments, etc. In a two-hour meeting, reserve 15 minutes. In a three-hour meeting, reserve 20 minutes. In a day-long meeting, take the last 20 to 30 minutes.

During this time, you also need to review any issues that are in the "Parking Lot" and *not* solve them but find a time, place, and process for them (please see Parking Lot in the Toolbox section).

If you build in review time, people will feel some psychological closure about the meeting and not leave feeling there are a lot of loose ends, and you communicate that we are action orientated and hold people accountable.

26. "Rabbit Holes" and "Moonshots."

Before you start an important meeting where you know that you have talkative participants **or** there is a difference of opinion **or** you have some people who *love* to hear themselves talk (*don't you just love those guys?*) **or** you have folks who like to "theorize" and love an exchange of ideas, try to get the group to agree that they need to look out for "rabbit holes" and "moonshots." This will get their attention. Explain that "rabbit holes" occur when group members get bogged down in an inappropriate level of detail—the level of detail that does not help but hinders the group's decision or process. The reality is that most people know exactly what a rabbit hole looks and sounds like. It is debilitating, and they don't know what to do about it.

Getting people's agreement up front that "we" all have to watch out for rabbit holes is the best way to prevent them. Every participant can ask, "Are we in a rabbit hole right now?" or "It feels like we are going down a rabbit hole."

A "moonshot" is the opposite of a rabbit hole but just as deadly. That's when a participant wanders off and takes the conversation "to the moon." Often, they will signal this by actually saying, "I don't want to go off on a tangent but..." You must intervene right there before they take off! Gently remind them about the topic at hand and try to redirect their conversation to the actual discussion. If you find you are already in a moonshot (it happens quickly!), you can ask the "astronaut" a question: "Rod, could you help me understand how what you are saying is connected to what we are talking about currently?" **Do not use sarcasm** because it will only fuel the spaceship (e.g., "Well Bob, if you only understood the complexities of this topic, you would clearly understand the connection") and off they go!

You can also suggest that we "park" their idea in the "Parking Lot" (see Toolbox section) or "Grass Catcher" and keep things moving. Once again, convey respect at all times, or you can create a situation that is hard to get out of.

(We have one client who actually has cut outs of a rabbit and a moon. They use them to quietly signal to others in the group where they think the conversation is going. They have used this technique for several years and it has helped make their senior management meetings more effective.)

27. For the truly courageous!

The following are two rather dramatic but very effective group management techniques:

- We worked with a team of eight executives who made an agreement to cut down long-winded conversations. Their ground rule or agreement was if two members of the group hold up a red card, the person talking has to stop. They believed that if two members believed that the discussion was wandering or off track, it was enough to pause and check things out.

  It might be noted that this group has very positive group culture, so the cards were not used to antagonize each other or stop debate. The cards signaled to the group that at least two members thought the discussion should come to an end.

- Another group we worked with had a verbal "weed whacker" signal to indicate that the conversation was going "into the weeds." Either too much detail or tangential thinking could trigger someone in the group to gently imitate a weed whacker. It was a humorous but very effective way to remind the talker that he or she was in the weeds.

References and Resources

References

1. Block, P. (2009). *Community: The structure of belonging.* San Francisco, CA: Berrett-Koehler.

2. Buzan, T. (1991). *Use both sides of your brain.* New York: Plume.

3. Chrislip, D. (2002). *The collaborative leadership feedback—A guide for citizens and civic leaders.* San Francisco, CA: Jossey-Bass.

4. Goldsmith, M. (2000). *Coaching for leadership: The practice of leadership coaching from the world's leading coaches.* San Francisco, CA: Jossey-Bass.

5. Gregorc, A. (2006). *The mind styles model: Theory, principles and application.* AFC.

6. Kaner, S., & colleagues. (2007). *Facilitator's guide to participatory decision making.* San Francisco, CA: Jossey-Bass, p. 32.

7. Kolb, D. (1984). *Experiential learning: Experience as the source of learning and development.* Englewood Cliffs, NJ: Prentice-Hall.

8. Owen, H. (1997). *Open space technology, a user's guide.* San Francisco, CA: Berrett-Koehler.

9. Sanaghan, P. (2009). *Collaborative strategic planning in higher education.* Washington, D.C.: NACUBO.

10. Sanaghan, Goldstein, & Conway. (2008). *The highly effective meeting profile.* Amherst, MA: HRD Press.

Resources

Benzilger Thinking Style Assessment—www.benzilger.org

Open Space—www.openspaceworld.org

Herrmann Brain Dominance Instrument (HBDI)—www.hbdi.com

Freemind—www.freemind.sourceforge.net

Mindjet—www.mindjet.com

— About the Authors —

Patrick Sanaghan, Ed.D., is president of The Sanaghan Group, an organizational consulting firm that specializes in strategic planning, leadership development, executive team building, meeting facilitation, and leadership transitions. He has worked in hundreds of organizations over the past 25 years.

The Sanaghan Group clients have included Saudi Aramco, Cornell University, Shell Oil, Barclay Capital, PSE&G, IBM, The Pennsylvania Ballet, The Parallax Hedge Fund, and the cabinet of the governor of Pennsylvania. Patrick serves on the board of The Lopez-Low Foundation and the Wheeled Scotsman.

Patrick speaks and writes frequently on leadership and strategic planning. He is the author of numerous articles and has co-authored several books on strategic planning, high-performing teams, and change management. His most recent book, *Collaborative Strategic Planning with Higher Education*, was published in 2009.

Dr. Paulette Gabriel is president of Key Leadership. An expert in executive development, organizational change, and transformation and team development, Paulette has a successful practice helping organizations and individuals accelerate their capacity for strategic alignment, development, self-renewal, and continuous learning.

Paulette has developed a model—Authentic Transforming Leadership—derived from a four-year study focused on how personal transformation impacts transformational leadership. Her research has enabled leaders to better understand how to capitalize on pivotal experiences so that who they are and what they do as leaders are indistinguishable.